UNLEAVENED FAITH

To Know
and
Understand

In Christ Jesus

D. PAUL WALKER

So they read in the book in the law of God distinctly, and gave the sense, and caused them to understand the reading.

Nehemiah 8:8

Photos Obtained Though

Adobe Stock
iStockphoto
Pixabay
Shutterstock
Unsplash
Public Domain

ISBN: 978-0-9797916-0-4
0-9797916-0-X

This and all my studies are based solely on the Authorized Version of 1611 commonly called the King James Version. All Scripture quotes unless otherwise noted are from the AV 1611 (KJV).

All *italicized* or **bold** print is added by the author for emphasis.

There is no English in the world equal to that found in the 1611 Bible ... Whether the original text was inspired or not, I have never felt any doubt as to the divine inspiration of the version of 1611.

William Lyon Phelps (1865-1943)
Reading the Bible, The Mackmillan Co., 1919
Lampson professor of English literature at Yale

THE FORBIDDEN BOOK
God's Holy Word was Prized
When 'Twas Unsafe to Read It?

Contents

UNLEAVENED FAITH
To Know and Understand

PREFACE

For there are many unruly and vain talkers and deceivers, specially they of the circumcision: Whose mouths must be stopped, who subvert whole houses, teaching things which they ought not, for filthy lucre's sake.

—TITUS 1:10-11

The Bible is the most published, sold, given away, personally owned, outlawed, read, neglected, loved, hated, praised, despised, book ever to have existed. It is esteemed as the very words of God, renounced as merely the work of men, cherished as truth, and scorned as fable. It promises peace beyond understanding but with trials and tribulation to all who trust in and live its precepts. It warns of false prophets, false apostles, false teachers, of Satan and his ministers appearing as an angel of light and ministers of righteousness—all deceiving and misleading on what the Bible says and means. It is quite a book. If what it says is true, all the contradictions and confusion over and about it are to be expected.

It is a book that admonishes mankind to have charity toward all, to recompense to no man evil for evil, provide things honest in the sight of all men, to love and care for your family and others as yourself. In short, there is no reason to disparage and reject the Bible nor the *God* of the Bible, except for the fact that many hate the idea that the God of the Bible is going to bring all things into judgment. Nevertheless, the Bible not only warns of that judgment but provides the means for all who will turn to its God to pass that judgment justified and guiltless.

Understandably, all men without the saving grace revealed in its pages fail that judgment as the Bible presents the strictest of religions in that it requires absolute sinless perfection to be saved. Unlike other religions that leave you hanging, unsure, as to whether you are good enough, the Bible tells us flat out—we are not. We can stand securely and confidently on this solid ground, the knowledge that we are not good enough, cannot save ourselves, next to God *"we are all as an unclean thing, and all our righteousnesses are as filthy rags."* With this knowledge, we can do what no other religion affords. It affords us the ability to see within its pages that the God of the Bible, the God of creation, the God of justice, judgment, and loving-kindness, has freely provided absolute sinless perfection for us: on the one condition that we believe him.

1

Numbers 14:11 And the LORD said unto Moses, How long will this people provoke me? and how **long will it be ere they believe me**,

Acts 24:14 But this I confess unto thee, that after the way which they call heresy, so worship I the God of my fathers, **believing all things which are written in the law and in the prophets**:

"Believing all things which are written," what should our attitude be toward the things that are written, God's word?

Psalms 138:2 I will worship toward thy holy temple, and praise thy name for thy lovingkindness and for thy truth: for **thou hast magnified thy word above all thy name**.

"Thou hast magnified thy word above all thy name." How much glory and honor is God placing upon his word by magnifying it above his name?

Deuteronomy 28:58 If thou wilt not observe to do all the words of this law that are written in this book, that thou mayest fear this **glorious and fearful name**, THE LORD THY GOD;

Psalms 111:9 He sent redemption unto his people: he hath commanded his covenant for ever: **holy and reverend is his name**.

Psalms 29:2 Give unto the LORD the **glory due unto his name**; worship the LORD in the beauty of holiness.

Psalms 148:13 Let them praise the name of the LORD: for **his name alone is excellent**; his glory is above the earth and heaven.

It is sure, many more verses extolling God's name could be listed. It is glorious and fearful; his name alone is excellent and reverend. It must now be asked, if God's name is glorious, to be praised, and to be reverenced, what is our attitude supposed to be toward his word which he not only puts but magnifies above his name?

> You Christians look after a document containing enough dynamite to blow all civilization to pieces, turn the world upside down and bring peace to a battle-torn planet. But you treat it as though it is nothing more than a piece of literature.
>
> —Mahatma Gandhi (1869-948);
> Leader of the Indian independence movement

Unleavened Faith is a series of studies that is all about believing and accepting what God said, letting the Bible speak for itself.

> Make the word of God as much as possible its own interpreter. You will best understand the word of God by comparing it with itself. *"Comparing spiritual things with spiritual."*
>
> —Sir Isaac Newton (1642-1727);
> English Physicist & Mathematician

It is taken without reservation that God wrote and preserved to this day his word. This book does not cover the controversy of which Bible; suffice it to say that God is not producing the multiple new versions that are being published year after year. Without apology, the studies herein are based on the 1611 Authorized Version of the Bible, commonly called the King James Version.

The studies presented here are written to and for the common man. You will not find words such as hermeneutics, Epistemology, Exegesis, Soteriology, or any such vanities, contained within them. Nor, except for minor things as the meaning of a name, will the Greek and Hebrew be relied upon to understand the English of our Bible.

> And it is the English Bible we are thinking about, the Bible in the vernacular, the tongue most of us best understand. One is grateful to have studied Hebrew and Greek, just to be able to tell others who have not that they do not require either to hearken to our Heavenly Father's voice. He has an advantage as a scholar who can utilize the original tongues; but the Bible was not given to scholars, but to the people, and *"hear we every man in our own tongue wherein we were born"* (Acts 2:8).
>
> [1]James M. Gray, D.D., How to Master the English Bible,
> The Winona Publishing Co. (1904)

2 Corinthians 3:12 Seeing then that we have such hope, **we use great plainness of speech**:

Although, there are those *"Whose mouths must be stopped, who subvert whole houses, teaching things which they ought not,"* it is not the purpose of these studies to judge any man or his motives but to speak the truth as God has given me light to see it and whatever any individual does with it, God will judge. These studies compare the teachings and doctrines as taught to what the Bible teaches. Individuals knowing the truth, through a personal knowledge of what the Bible says, is the only way to stop the mouths that need to be stopped. So with Christian charity for all, I present these studies of the doctrines of Scripture for your consideration. If studied with a heart's desire to learn and understand God's word it is felt that the truth will shine through.

I realize that we are in the last days and that many, even those who have never studied or read the Bible, are having their interest piqued by books and preaching on the Lord's return, the Tribulation, and end of the world. Knowing the exact time and day of his return will not make you a better Christian or witness for him. Knowing the doctrines and teachings of Scripture will.

I hope you will enjoy these studies as much as I have enjoyed preparing them.

KNOW
YOUR
PLACE

World Religions

Pure religion and undefiled before God and the Father is this, To visit the fatherless and widows in their affliction, and to keep himself unspotted from the world.

—*JAMES* 1:27

To begin a study of God's word it is best to start by finding our place within the world of religion in general. It is affirmed by some, saved by the grace of God through the shed blood of Jesus Christ, that they do not have a religion; they have salvation. I would agree with that to an extent. Salvation is obtained by a belief. Religion will be looked at here in this broadest sense as simply beliefs held. An examination of religion on this level will lead us to a noteworthy truth.

The world is full of different beliefs on God, spirituality, theology, etc. By any loose definition, there are hundreds of distinct belief systems. Below are illustrations of some of the more prominent.

In searching for the right one as opposed to the wrong one, the vast number of religions is a huge stumbling block. It is just too many for the common man to manage; just two are needed, the one or the other, to be able to choose. This leads us to the study of comparative religion.

Comparative Religion

I call heaven and earth to record this day against you, that I have set before you life and death, blessing and cursing: therefore choose life, that both thou and thy seed may live:

—*Deuteronomy* 30:19

There are those that actually spend their time in the pursuit of the study of comparative religions. Be thankful for them. Whoever these fine fellows happen to be they have performed a tremendous amount of work for us in having tracked and studied the religions of the world comparing, categorizing, and organizing them into twenty-two groups. Here are the groups listed by the number of adherents.

1. Christianity: 2.1 billion
2. Islam: 1.5 billion
3. Secular/Nonreligious/Agnostic/Atheist: 1.1 billion
4. Hinduism: 900 million
5. Chinese traditional religion: 394 million
6. Buddhism: 376 million
7. primal-indigenous: 300 million
8. African Traditional and Diasporic: 100 million
9. Sikhism: 23 million
10. Juche: 19 million
11. Spiritism: 15 million
12. Judaism: 14 million
13. Baha'i: 7 million
14. Jainism: 4.2 million
15. Shinto: 4 million
16. Cao Dai: 4 million
17. Zoroastrianism: 2.6 million
18. Tenrikyo: 2 million
19. Neo-Paganism: 1 million
20. Unitarian-Universalism: 800 thousand
21. Rastafarianism: 600 thousand
22. Scientology: 500 thousand

Although all the religions of the world have been categorized into twenty-two categories, it is still far from what the average student of religion or Bible is able to distill in determining the right one from the wrong one, the one from the other.

In a final attempt to narrow the distinctions between religions, those resolute undiscouraged fine fellows have reduced that number to five major groupings containing all the religions of the world based on the criteria of how they perceive or conceive of God.

1. Hindu Type—Polytheistic, many gods and/or goddesses
2. Buddhist Type—Atheistic, no God
3. New Age Spiritualistic—Man is or will be God
4. Islamic Type—God is Unknowable
5. Christian Type—God is Knowable and desires to be known

These can also be listed as the following using the criteria of how God is perceived or conceived of. It may be determined as one deems fit to place a particular religion into any of the five categories.

1. Many Gods
2. No God
3. Man is God
4. Unknowable God
5. Knowable God

Who did the original research is unknown; certainly, they were not all Bible-believing Christians? Nonetheless, their work turns out to be rather miraculous in that these five groups are the five categories of religion found within the Scriptures.

Five Major Religions groups referenced in the Bible:

Many Gods

Jeremiah 11:13 For **according to the number of thy cities were thy gods**, O Judah;

Isaiah 2:8 Their land also is **full of idols**;

No God

Psalms 14:1 The fool hath said in his heart, **There is no God.**

Man is God

Ezekiel 28:2 Son of man, say unto the prince of Tyrus, Thus saith the Lord GOD; Because thine heart is lifted up, and **thou hast said, I am a God, I sit in the seat of God, in the midst of the seas; yet thou art a man, and not God**, though thou set thine heart as the heart of God:

Unknowable God

Acts 17:23 For as I passed by, and beheld your devotions, I found an altar with this inscription, **TO THE UNKNOWN GOD.** Whom therefore ye ignorantly worship, him declare I unto you.

Knowable God

> *Jeremiah 9:24* But let him that glorieth glory in this, **that he understandeth and knoweth me**, that I am the LORD which exercise lovingkindness, judgment, and righteousness, in the earth: for in these things I delight, saith the LORD.

It is far easier to deal with five than hundreds and much better than twenty-two. However, our quest is to narrow our choice down to two, the right one and the wrong one. Meditating on this conundrum without the vast number of choices a dividing line can be seen between these groups; using different criteria these five can be combined into two. Now two is a number that can be handled as we are looking for just two religions—the one or the other.

If the criterion is changed from their perception of God, which gave us five categories to their scheme for progression, the number of categories can be reduced. By progression, I mean their method for moving up, whether it is termed salvation, nirvana, becoming one with the universe, obtaining a better reincarnation, etc. In biblical terms, what is their plan of salvation? Under this criterion, there are only two choices.

The first choice, by man's own efforts, his works, his self-righteousness, earned or received as payment for a debt owed to him. The second, by the grace of God, received as a free gift, without works.

You could use different terms to denote the two columns:

Works	Gift
Self-righteousness	God's righteousness
Debt\Earned	Grace
Do	Done

For our purposes, the column heads used from here on will be the biblical terms "works" versus. "grace."

It is evident, that the two theological extremes are mutually exclusive.

> *Romans 11:6* And **if by grace, then is it no more of works**: otherwise grace is no more grace. But **if it be of works, then is it no more grace**: otherwise work is no more work.

> *Romans 4:4* Now to him that worketh is the reward **not reckoned of grace, but of debt**.

Where does faith come in?

> *Romans 4:16* Therefore **it is of faith, that it might be by grace**;

12

If you are graciously given a free gift with a payment book attached, it is not gracious, free, nor a gift. Adding works disannuls grace, free, and gift.

> *Galatians 5:4* Christ is become of no effect unto you, whosoever of you are justified by the law; **ye are fallen from grace**.

> *Romans 4:14* For if they which are of the law be heirs, **faith is made void, and the promise made of none effect**:

Biblically, works refer to establishing self-righteousness denoted by keeping the law of God, doing good, etc. There is a teaching that putting faith in Christ would be a work; therefore, faith cannot be internal but the gift of God. This is totally unbiblical. Biblical definitions must be used; in the Bible, works and grace/faith are mutually exclusive. Putting our faith in Christ is not works as defined by the Scriptures.[1]

There are two facets, two sides of the same coin, when it comes to the religion of works. Both equate to self-righteousness: (1) keeping the law, (2) proclaiming innocents, having done nothing to be condemn for. It is often expressed as pure self-righteousness, "I'm a good person. I've never killed anybody. I treat others as I want to be treated. Why should God condemn me?"

> *Luke 18:11* The Pharisee stood and prayed thus with himself, God, I thank thee, that **I am not as** other **men are, extortioners, unjust, adulterers, or even as this publican**.

Then there is the expanded definition of works that of doing penance, voluntary self-punishment, to pay for or cover one's sins, or to atone for some wrongdoing. This can take on many forms from reciting prayers to substantial self-abuse. Penance is a large part of religion by works.

When comparing the world's religions by the parameters of their individual plan or method of progression, salvation, upward mobility, or whatever term is used, it becomes obvious that the progression of biblical Christianity—by grace through faith and not of ourselves not of works—is a religion that is unique among the world's religions. It stands unequaled, distinct, unparalleled, among all the world's religions, which are works based. Biblical Christianity is exceptional, uncommon, peculiar.

---

[1] See section: "Faith or Works", under Precepts

The One or the Other

And if it seem evil unto you to serve the LORD, choose you this day whom ye will serve; whether the gods which your fathers served that were on the other side of the flood, or the gods of the Amorites, in whose land ye dwell: but as for me and my house, we will serve the LORD.

—JOSHUA 24:15

Success, all religions of the world have been concentrated down to two. There are only two religions in the world—the one or the other, the wrong or the right. They are quite easy to tell apart. The one is based on man's works; the other is not of man's works. The one says to rely on yourself, find yourself, heal yourself, clean yourself. The other says you are lost, incurable, filthy. The one says you have time; it will all work out in the end. The other says today, now. The one is a struggle, a constant effort; the other is a gift bringing peace, the product of grace and mercy. The one will make a few allowances, nobody is perfect; the other demands the sinless perfection that you can never provide and—provides it for you.

The one or the other, the wrong or the right one; how to choose? The easy answer to that question is to look in a mirror.

Proverbs 20:9 Who can say, **I have made my heart clean, I am pure from my sin**?

It is your decision, your choice. Are you righteous, holy, clean, pure? Contemplate just your thoughts over the last week. If you are able to make yourself pure, choose the one; if you are not able to wash yourself clean and pure of your sins, choose the other.

Romans 6:23 For **the wages of sin is death**; but **the gift of God is eternal life through Jesus Christ our Lord**.

"By grace are ye saved through faith, and that not of yourselves: it is the gift of God, not of works" is a singular unique religion separate from all the religions of the world. This is where the contention arises. All the religions of the world can come together without condemning each other as they are all the same religion; that of man's own efforts. On the other hand, you have a religion that condemns all the rest—by grace through faith.

At this point, it must also be noted that there are those that pervert the gospel of grace through faith and teach a doctrine of works in whole or in part as Christian doctrine. This will be covered later in our studies. Suffice it, for now, to say that as much as they try to mix Christianity with and make it just another religion of works, they are sadly mistaken. As reference earlier, grace and works are mutually exclusive.

By grace through faith is not the only thing unique about the other religion. Its God is also unique among the gods, one true living God, ever-existing, knowable and wanting to be known, gracious and merciful. There is also one unique book that leads us in the way of all truth. The Bible is unique among all the world's religious writings. There is also one unique Bible among all the contenders for the title of God's word—the AV 1611. This is covered by many in other studies and books, but to show its uniqueness one point to remember is that no one will say that they are holding in their hands the inerrant persevered word of God unless they are holding an Authorized Version of 1611.

In closing, it would be beneficial to look at the world's religions from another vantage point and see some of what the God of the Bible has delivered us from.

Catholic—flagellation

Islamic—flagellation

Hindu/Taoism—hanging from fishhooks and self-mutilation. Self-mutilation is quite normal in ceremonies for religions based on works.

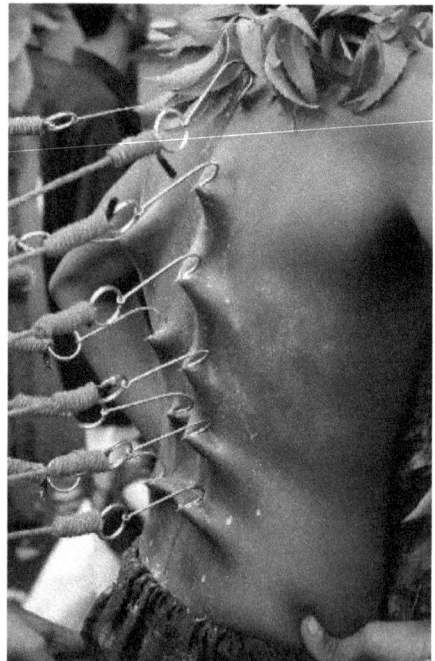

African Traditional Scarring

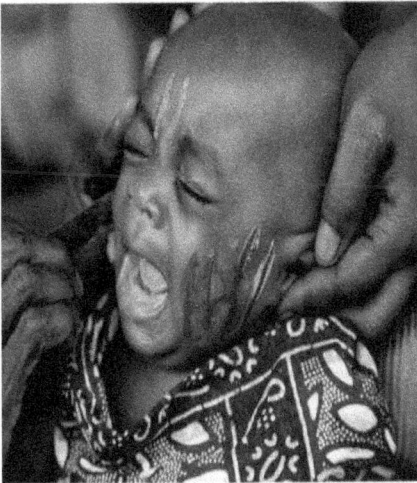

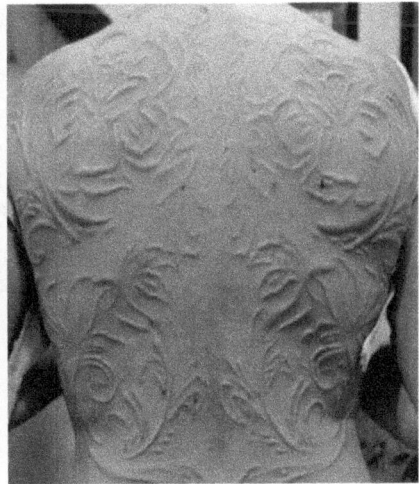

The above are on the extreme end of works usually found where the religion is not only dominant but holding political power as well. The extremes have not been seen in the USA up to now for that reason.

As stated above, all the religions of the world, except for biblical Christianity, are all the same: a religion of self, self-righteousness, and self-glorification. They are just the opposite of biblical Christianity's glorification of God.

> Ephesians 2:8 For **by grace are ye saved through faith**; and that **not of yourselves**: **it is the gift of God**:

It is the religion of works that the God of the Bible has saved us from. The God of the Bible forbids the practice of self-mutilation and physical abuse as penance or a show of earnestness in one's devotion. It also forbids many other practices like widows being burnt alive along with their husband's corpse, sacrificing children, crawling on your hands and knees over rough stone, and many other religious/cultural customs that permeate the religion of works. Most importantly, the religion of the Bible relieves us from the impossible requirement to obtain and maintain self-righteousness and gives us God's righteousness.

> 1 Kings 18:28 (Prophets of Baal) And they cried aloud, and **cut themselves after their manner with knives and lancets**, till **the blood gushed** out upon them.

When questioned about other religions, it is safe to say that there are only two: one of works, the other of grace.

This is as far as reason alone can take us; to grow further in the knowledge of God and his ways the light of his revelations must be relied upon. So we begin our series of studies of the Bible, its religion, and the true intent and meaning of our faith, unleavened, to obtain a greater understanding and to fulfill our place as children of the Most High.

> Matthew 16:6 Then Jesus said unto them, **Take heed and beware of the leaven** of the Pharisees and of the Sadducees.

THE CHURCH

Church Types

**And no marvel; for Satan himself is transformed
into an angel of light. Therefore it is no great thing
if his ministers also be transformed as the
ministers of righteousness; whose end shall be
according to their works.**

—2 *CORINTHIANS 11:14-15*

Our study of comparative religions has shown there are only two religions in the world, the right one and the wrong one. They should be quite easy to tell apart. The wrong one is based wholly or in part on man's works in obtaining or maintaining salvation. The right one is not of man's works; it demands perfect sinless perfection. Most importantly, it provides it for you as a gift from God.

As those who have trusted in Christ Jesus, we now know where our place is in the world; our religion is peculiar, unique, and separate. Confident in this knowledge, it is now time to turn our attention to the study of our religion, that which is called Christianity.

Within that which is called Christian many competing doctrinal teachings that must be rightly divided exist. One of the main dividing points is whether they hold to the gospel of grace through faith without works or one of works.

The first concept that must be accepted and understood is that we have an enemy that has an alternate Church opposed to the true one.

> *2 Corinthians 11:13-15* For such are **false apostles**, **deceitful workers**, transforming themselves into the apostles of Christ. [14]And no marvel; for **Satan himself is transformed into an angel of light**. [15]Therefore it is no great thing if **his ministers also be transformed as the ministers of righteousness**; whose end shall be according to their works.

Satan is not overly concerned with barrooms, drug dens, atheist, agnostics, etc.; the flesh in action is damning many quite nicely. He may help it along, but his desire is to be worshiped even if it is in ignorance.

> *Acts 17:23* For as I passed by, and beheld your devotions, I found an altar with this inscription, TO THE UNKNOWN GOD. Whom therefore **ye ignorantly worship**, him declare I unto you.

> *1 Corinthians 10:20* But I say, that the things which the Gentiles sacrifice, **they sacrifice to devils, and not to God**: and I would not that ye should have fellowship with devils.

From this desire to supplant and usurp the glory that only belongs to God an imitation or alternate type of Church was implemented. These

20

two church types have been designated by various names by different commentators. Here, I will define them as the Institutional-type church and the Biblical-type church.

There are pure Institutional churches as well as churches that have been corrupted by mixing within themselves various aspects of the institutional. The most prominent feature differing these two church types is that salvation is obtained in the institutional type by an individual's association and standing within the institution. The institution mediates between man and God and dispenses God's grace and forgiveness granted by a sacramental system: a system of works. Whereas salvation within the biblical type solely depends on an individual's relationship with God based on the direct mediation and atonement of Christ Jesus alone and one's own faith in the gospel.

> The most prominent feature of the Church (institutional) -type is the stress it lays on the institutional character of the Church which is thought of as being in exclusive possession of the supernatural life. It thinks of the Church as the Body of Christ and as an extension of the Incarnation and, therefore, in possession of a life and tradition which carry within themselves a certain divine authority. It conveys its divine life to the individual by means of its sacramental system.[2]

The most recognizable fully functioning institutional-type church called Christian is Roman Catholicism. Nevertheless, there are smaller denominations and independent churches that practice their own variety of institutionalism, for example, claiming that you have to be a member of their denomination to be saved making it, the institution, the vehicle of grace.

The biblical-type Church is a body of individuals having a personal relationship with God through faith in the atoning sacrifice of Christ Jesus. There is no intermediary between man and God except for Christ himself. You enter the biblical-type church only through a personal choice based on a conscious conversion at an age when you can make that choice.

1 Timothy 2:5 For there is one God, and **one mediator between God and men**, the man Christ Jesus;

The biblical-type church is a free-will association; in the institutional-type, it is your relationship to the institution; you must be put into the church, the institution, hence requirements such as infant-baptism bringing the child under the supernatural influence of it. In the one, the institution is the church and your salvation depends on your standing within it; in the other, the believers are the Church; your salvation is in your relationship to God through Christ Jesus alone.

---

[2]A. C. Underwood, D.D., Forerunners, A History of the English Baptists, The Baptist Union of Great Britain and Ireland

In the forward to the book Forerunners, A History of the English Baptists is an excellent detailed description of the two types of Churches. It is highly recommended reading and required knowledge for the student of the Bible (see the appendix). This book is referenced here not to extol Baptist but for its exceptional explanation of the church types.

The institutional-type church is religion used for political ends, to control a people. Most all of the world's religions that are not faithful to biblical Christianity are political in this aspect, whether to appease the pride of an individual or to make the people unwilling pawns in controlling the wealth and resources of a nation.

With this understanding, the following studies are concerned with rightly dividing the word of truth thereby rightly dividing all else. They will compare that which is called Christian with God's word.

2 Timothy 2:15 **Study** to shew thyself approved unto God, a workman that needeth not to be ashamed, **rightly dividing the word of truth.**

SEVEN
PRECEPTS
TO
UNDERSTANDING
THE
BIBLE

INTRODUCTION

**For God is not
the author of confusion,
but of peace**

—1 CORINTHIANS 14:33

**Knowing this first,
that no prophecy of the scripture
is of any private interpretation.**

—2 PETER 1:20

Order in life, as in all things, necessitates borders, boundaries, and rules all built upon a base set of principles. These principles are the general truths, the accepted conventions, the precepts, that all else is founded upon. During the course of my studies, I have found that there are seven biblical precepts that constitute a framework for biblical understanding. God is the author of order; order is necessary to understanding.

As it is in life, and all creation, so it is when it comes to the study of God's word. There must also be order, rules to govern a proper understanding and comprehension of its teachings and doctrines. These rules are in opposition to private interpretations which give no regard to any such guiding limitations. The biblical precepts are simply God's stated principles or the general truths on how he has determined and established all things. No doctrine or teaching can be correct if it attempts to evade or fails to conform to any one of them.

Psalms 119:100 I understand more than the ancients, because **I keep thy precepts**.

These seven precepts, if understood and adhered to, will bring order and discernment to aid in correctly interpreting the precepts, teachings, and doctrines of Scripture. These principles are not a new discovery on my part. They have been taught individually by many; several authors have written whole books on at least one. However, I have never seen them listed together or taught as a complete cognitive list, a single unit. They act as a guide to meditation and, more importantly, limits to the imagination in studying the Scriptures. This study merely sets them in order so that they may be recognized as such a unit, a set of rules to study and judge by.

I earnestly believe that an understanding of these seven precepts and faithfully keeping them as a guide is the secret to unlocking the meaning and wonder of the Bible. It has been many years, many hundreds of conversations, and debates, since I first began, in 1993, to teach these precepts as a list. With the passing of each, I am ever more convinced of their worth. To study the Scriptures without an understanding of these principles is to travel a highway haphazardly marked with partial or no signposts, a highway such as I hope none of my readers desire to travel.

24

These seven precepts are not esoteric, not difficult to grasp in and of themselves. It is quite comforting to have such guides. The seven are divided into two parts. The first three deal with the human heart, one's attitude and desire toward the Scriptures. The last four deal with the construction of the Scriptures, how the Bible is written and to be correctly interpreted. I hope that you will find them as useful as I have.

> So great is my veneration for the Bible, that the earlier my children begin to read it the more confident will be my hope that they will prove useful citizens to their country and respectable members of society.

—J. Q. Adams (1767-1848)
6th President of the United States

THE ATTITUDE
OF THE HEART

Blessed are they that keep his testimonies, and that seek him with the whole heart.

—PSALMS 119:2

1) **Diligence**
2) **Neither Add Nor Diminish**
3) **Believe All That Is Written**

And if you will stop and ask yourself, why you are not as pious as the primitive Christians were, your own heart will tell you, that it is neither through ignorance, nor inability, but purely because you never thoroughly intended it.

—William Law (1686-1761) English clergy

Diligence

But without faith it is impossible to please him: for he that cometh to God must believe that he is, and that he is a rewarder of them that diligently seek him.

—*Hebrews 11:6*

A common response when speaking with people is that they had tried to read the Bible at one time, but not having immediate comprehension, the Bible was set aside and left to collect dust. This type of statement always betrays one's heart attitude. This is especially true when it is from professionals, businessmen, college graduates, tradesmen of all sorts; men who have and continue to diligently study the disciplines of this world to reap its rewards but apply no time, no effort, no diligence, in the study of God's word. Men have their priorities reversed. They spend all their time preparing for and attempting to profit in the here and now, our short and temporary home; they give no time preparing to profit in eternity, our long and permanent home.

> *Ecclesiastes 12:5* Also when they shall be afraid of that which is high, and fears shall be in the way, and the almond tree shall flourish, and the grasshopper shall be a burden, and desire shall fail: because **man goeth to his long home**, and the mourners go about the streets:

Whether or not due *diligence* is given to the study of the Bible is determined by the heart, its attitude toward God and his word. To understand the Bible, a godly perspective of life's priorities and a heart's desire to seek the Lord is required. How should the time devoted to the study of the words of our Creator be compared to the time spent in the pursuit of the profit and pleasures of this world? God is *"a rewarder of them that diligently seek him."*

> *Jeremiah 9:23-24* Thus saith the LORD, Let not the wise man glory in his wisdom, neither let the mighty man glory in his might, let not the rich man glory in his riches: [24]**But let him that glorieth glory in this, that he understandeth and knoweth me**, that I am the LORD which exercise lovingkindness, judgment, and righteousness, in the earth: for in these things I delight, saith the LORD.

The word "diligent," "diligence," or "diligently" appears 62 times in 61 verses in the Bible. All but a few refer to being diligent toward obeying God's word, diligent in studying God's word, or diligent in preparing ourselves to serve him.

> *Exodus 15:26* If thou wilt **diligently hearken to the voice of the LORD** thy God, and wilt do that which is right in his sight...

Deuteronomy 4:9 Only take heed to thyself, and **keep thy soul diligently**, lest thou forget the things which thine eyes have seen, and lest they depart from thy heart all the days of thy life: ...

Deuteronomy 6:7 And thou shalt **teach them diligently** unto thy children, ...

It is important to conceptualize the abstract meaning of diligence and make it a concrete desire of the heart to meet the standard that will be rewarded by God. The following is a short word study on diligence. It is not necessary to memorize the following definitions, but it will be extremely helpful to familiarize yourself with the terms and comprehend the action that each describes so that you understand what God is requiring, what he will reward.

Diligence {Latin—diligo, to love earnestly}

- Persistent application to one's work or duty; persevering effort
- Due attention; proper heed; care; steady application
- Exertion of body and/or mind without delay or sloth
- Constant and close attention to

Constancy is an interesting part of diligence in relation to God's word.

Constancy {Latin—consto, to stand}

- Fixedness, standing firm
- Unchanging; immutable
- A permanent state; lasting affection
- Particularly applicable to firmness of mind under sufferings to steadiness in attachments

If time is taken to study and consider the above list, it will be seen that the substance of these words are not physical attributes, not all mental attributes, but all are qualities of the heart. Persistence is not by strength but by a heart's desire; you persevere when physical strength and mental determination fail. Zeal from the heart is undampened by disappointment while the affections of the flesh fade as fast as they are obtained; our thoughts change constantly. Lasting affections and steadfastness are qualities of the heart and are anchored to its desire. Standing firm, fixedness, unchanging, are attributes of God that he desires us to have.

Malachi 3:6 For I am the LORD, **I change not**; ...

James 1:17 the Father of lights, with whom is **no variableness, neither shadow of turning**.

28

Hebrews 13:8 Jesus Christ **the same yesterday, and to day, and for ever**.

Daniel 6:26 the God of Daniel: ... he is the living God, and **steadfast for ever,**

1 Corinthians 15:58 Therefore, my beloved brethren, **be ye steadfast, unmoveable**, always abounding in the work of the Lord, forasmuch as ye know that your labour is not in vain in the Lord.

2 Thessalonians 2:15 Therefore, brethren, **stand fast**, and hold the traditions which ye have been taught, whether by word, or our epistle.

Do you have a desire to know God, to understand his word? Make that desire a permanent state, a lasting affection. God is not going to give the undecided, the lackadaisical, the double-minded, nor those that are self-promoting, any considerable understanding or wisdom in his word.

Psalms 78:8 And might not be as their fathers, a stubborn and rebellious generation; a generation that **set not their heart aright**, and **whose spirit was not stedfast with God**.

James 4:8 **purify your hearts**, ye double minded.

James 1:8 A double minded man is unstable in all his ways.

Philippians 2:21 For **all seek their own**, not the things which are Jesus Christ's.

There is much more to the admonition that God *"is a rewarder of them that diligently seek him"* than first meets the eye. The Bible is our lamp, our light, and our guide; without a knowledge of what it says the Scriptures cannot be understood nor can life, history, or the nature of the universe, be understood correctly. The greatest indignity man as part of creation can perform toward God, the Creator, is not to listen and diligently consider when he speaks, to forsake his word and walk in our own way.

Psalms 10:4 The wicked, through the pride of his countenance, will not seek after God: **God is not in all his thoughts**.

2 Corinthians 10:5 Casting down imaginations, and every high thing that exalteth itself against the knowledge of God, and **bringing into captivity every thought** to the obedience of Christ;

1 Samuel 2:6-8 The LORD **killeth, and maketh alive**: he **bringeth down to the grave, and bringeth up**. [7]The LORD **maketh poor, and maketh rich**: he **bringeth low, and lifteth up**. [8]He **raiseth up the poor out of the dust**, and **lifteth up the beggar from the dunghill**, to set them among princes, and to make them inherit the throne of glory: for **the pillars of the earth are the LORD'S**, and he hath set the world upon them.

According to the Scriptures, there is nothing that is without the Lord, nor is there anything not in his control. It is far better advice to diligently seek him and an understanding of his word than the wisdom and understanding of this world.

The first precept to understanding the Bible is:

God is a rewarder of them
that Diligently seek him

Some believers stop looking for treasure in their Bibles after a while. They don't stick to the map, don't rely on the Word to chart their course, and after a while, they get detoured into a maze of self-help books, psychology, intellectual speculation, philosophy, materialism, educational title mongering, mass media punditry, or motions of empty religiosity.

The Translator to the Reader
The Orthodox Jewish Bible
Artists for Israel International Publishing

Neither Add
Nor Diminish

Ye shall not add unto the word which I command you, neither shall ye diminish ought from it, that ye may keep the commandments of the LORD your God which I command you.

—DEUTERONOMY 4:2

On the face of it, this next precept would seem to be a self-evident simple truth, do not add to, nor diminish from the word of God. However, men and women are prone to adding and subtracting from the Bible almost subconsciously. The following familiar statements are less than biblically true:

- Cleanliness is next to godliness

- Finders keepers, losers weepers

- The Golden Rule as being, love your neighbor

Men have cut God out of the "Golden Rule" which should be the first, highest rule: Love God with all your heart and mind. The second rule is called the "Royal Law," love your neighbor as yourself.

> *James 2:8* If ye fulfil **the royal law** according to the scripture, Thou shalt **love thy neighbour as thyself,** ye do well:)

The violation of this precept takes on many forms from blatant out and out lies to feigned subtleties of those who contrive false representations, take out of context, and otherwise imitate the truth to form the multitudes of false teachings and doctrines struggled with today.

> *2 Peter 2:1-3* But there were false prophets also among the people, **even as there shall be false teachers among you**, who privily shall bring in damnable heresies, even denying the Lord that bought them, and bring upon themselves swift destruction. ²And many shall follow their pernicious ways; by reason of whom the way of truth shall be evil spoken of. 3And through covetousness shall **they with feigned words make merchandise of you**:

> *2 Corinthians 11:13-15* For such are false apostles, deceitful workers, transforming themselves into the apostles of Christ. ¹⁴And no marvel; for **Satan himself is transformed into an angel of light**. ¹⁵Therefore it is no great thing if **his ministers also be transformed as the ministers of righteousness**; whose end shall be according to their works.

It is unfortunate; however, I must keep my conscience clear and state that I believe the worst plague affecting the Church is not from the false but from within our own ranks.

Acts 20:29-30 For I know this, that after my departing shall grievous wolves enter in among you, not sparing the flock. [30]Also **of your own selves shall men arise, speaking perverse things, to draw away disciples after them**.

The acquisition of such absolute command over the consciences and understanding of a congregation, however obscure or despised by the world, is more truly grateful to the pride of the human heart, than the possession of the most despotic power, imposed by arms and conquest on a reluctant people.

Edward Gibbon Esq, History Of The Decline And Fall
Of The Roman Empire; Chapter XV (1776)

The precepts discussed in this study, understood and applied, will prevent the student of Scripture from being deceived. Failure to understand is derived from the infraction of the first precept, the lack of diligent study, from which improper conclusions are drawn. This leads to the formulation of incorrect doctrines, much of which are obtained by adding or diminishing from what the Bible says. A human quality is to trust its faulty reasoning and become fixated, mentally stuck on an erroneous idea or principle.

One error many people make is to learn something the wrong way and stick to it no matter what.
Harry Lorayne, Secrets of Mind Power (1961)

Being too dogmatic in attitude toward what is thought to be known can blind us to errors. Always be open-minded continually searching the Scriptures affirming or modifying our understanding, as necessary. There is always more to learn and those that have learned it. This is not to be tossed about *"with every wind of doctrine;"* it is self-examination, building upon the truths you have previously biblically discovered. Be firm in the knowledge of God's precepts with strict adherence to the context of God's word. Examine and reexamine everything as you study; growing in knowledge and understanding requires it. You can be well assured that at some point a modification or clarification of a belief or interpretation held will have to be made if you are growing at all.

Ephesians 4:14 That we henceforth **be no more children, tossed to and fro, and carried about with every wind of doctrine**, by the sleight of men, and cunning craftiness, whereby they lie in wait to deceive;

1 Timothy 5:17 Let the elders that rule well be counted worthy of double honour, **especially they who labour in the word and doctrine**.

Be wise in understanding that all men, and the ladies too, are naturally inclined to being slack, puffed up, and self-serving rather than diligently searching the Scriptures. Men change the Bible, wrest its passages, misquote, misapply, and dismiss; that is, they add and diminish from the

words of the Book. When we ought to be constantly adjusting our attitudes, way of thinking, values, priorities, so that they conform to the
word of God as we obtain greater knowledge and understanding in the
Scriptures, we are defiant, self-willed, obstinate. If we have trusted in the
Lord Jesus Christ, we should hold no principles, opinions, or attitudes,
that cannot be shown from the Bible, without adding thereto nor diminishing therefrom, to be correct.

Carefully consider the fact that this precept embodies more than just
the addition or removal of words within the Bible. It also includes changing the meaning or the sense of the words, as in not keeping to the context
of a passage or the use of proper grammar. These mental changes take
place before the words are changed.

> *Nehemiah 8:4-8* And Ezra the scribe stood upon a pulpit of wood,
> ...⁵And Ezra opened the book in the sight of all the people;
> ...⁷Also Jeshua, and Bani, ... and the Levites, caused the people
> to understand the law: and the people stood in their place. ⁸So **they
> read in the book in the law of God distinctly, and gave the
> sense, and caused them to understand the reading**.

Simply placing the wrong meaning on a word can lead to a false understanding of the doctrines and precepts of God. It is especially important to pick the proper meaning in accordance with its context, subject,
and cross-references. All the words in the Bible have understandable definitions and when held in the context in which they appear all but very
few are easily understood. A good dictionary is always a good investment;
however, the Bible will define words within itself. Beware of anyone who
offers their own private or theological definitions. Be especially wary of
those who based their definition in the shrouded mist of unrecorded history of ancient antiquity; context is everything—context, Context, CON-
TEXT!

Another all-too-common mistake is to assume a meaning where there
is none. It must be remembered that the smallest unit of English grammar,
or any other language, which has meaning is the sentence. Anything less
than a whole sentence—a clause, phrase, or any group of words—has no
significance outside the context of its sentence. It is an amazing feat of
ignorance when one bases their teaching on a mere phrase taken out of
the context of its sentence; many have done just that.

> *2 Peter 1:20* Knowing this first, that **no prophecy of the scripture
> is of any private interpretation**.

> *1 Peter 4:11* **If any man speak, let him speak as the oracles of
> God**; if any man minister, let him do it as of the ability which God
> giveth: **that God in all things may be glorified through Jesus
> Christ**, to whom be praise and dominion for ever and ever. Amen.

> *Deuteronomy 4:2* **Ye shall not add unto the word** which I
> command you, **neither shall ye diminish ought from it**, that ye

may keep the commandments of the LORD your God which I command you.

Proverbs 30:6 **Add thou not unto his words**, lest he reprove thee, and thou be found a liar.

The second precept to understanding the Bible is:

Ye shall not add unto the word
neither shall ye diminish ought from it

Make the word of God as much as possible its own interpreter. You will best understand the word of God by comparing it with itself. *"Comparing spiritual things with spiritual."*

Sir Isaac Newton (1642-1727)
English physicist and mathematician

Believe
All that is Written

But this I confess unto thee, that after the way which they call heresy, so worship I the God of my fathers, believing all things which are written in the law and in the prophets:

—*ACTS 24:14*

The Bible swirls in controversy but how complicated is all the hubbub? There are only three attitudes that can be held toward its pages: love, hate, or indifference. It is either God's word, it is not, or who cares.

Revelation 3:15-16 I know thy works, that thou art neither cold nor hot: I would thou wert cold or hot. [16]So then **because thou art lukewarm, and neither cold nor hot, I will spue thee out of my mouth**.

The worst that can be done is to be indifferent to the Bible; love it or hate it, but do not ignore it. God demands a side be picked. The wait-and-see what happens approach is more loathsome to God than out and out rejecting his word.

Matthew 27:49 The rest said, **Let be, let us see whether Elias will come to save him**.

God preserved his word, or we do not have his word: love it, hate it; the question is no more complicated than that. All the controversy and contention has never had anything to do with whether the Bible is God's word. It has always been about whether it is believed, not believed, or ignored, wait and see.

> God has determined that divine things should enter through the heart into the mind, and not through the mind into the heart. In divine things, therefore, it is necessary to love them in order to know them.
>
> Blaise Pascal (1623-1662) Christian, mathematician, physicist

Romans 4:3 For what saith the scripture? Abraham **believed God**, and it was counted unto him for righteousness.

Galatians 3:6-7 Even as **Abraham believed God**, and **it was accounted to him for righteousness**. [7]Know ye therefore that **they which are of faith**, the same are the children of Abraham.

Luke 24:25 Then he said unto them, O fools, and slow of heart **to believe all that the prophets have spoken**:

Many of the pulpits of the world are filled with men and women standing before their congregations and proclaiming their unbelief in the Scriptures. They disavow anything and everything that requires faith in the power of God by ascribing them to allegories, legend, or mythology.

Whether it be the Genesis account of creation, Noah's flood, dividing the Red Sea, or the person and resurrection of our Lord and Saviour, they *add and diminish* from the words, meaning, and sense of the Scriptures rejecting God's revelations.

> *John 3:12* If I have told you earthly things, and **ye believe not, how shall ye believe**, if tell you of heavenly things?

> *2 Timothy 3:5* Having a form of godliness, **but denying the power thereof: from such turn away**.

> *John 5:46-47* For **had ye believed Moses, ye would have believed me**: for he wrote of me. [47]But **if ye believe not** his writings, **how shall ye believe my words**?

What is the reason for this unbelief? Simply, they are men without faith. They stumble from the beginning in not believing God.

> *2 Thessalonians 3:2* for **all men have not faith**.

> *Deuteronomy 32:20* And he said, I will hide my face from them, I will see what their end shall be: for they are a very froward generation, **children in whom is no faith**.

> *Hebrews 11:3* **Through faith we understand** that the worlds were framed by the word of God, so that things which are seen were not made of things which do appear.

What is to be thought of those that reject the Scriptures as fact, whether they be scholar or novice? What does God's word say about such?

> *John 10:26* But **ye believe not**, because **ye are not of my sheep**, ...

> *Luke 16:29-31* They have Moses and the prophets; **let them hear them**. ...[31]And he said unto him, **If they hear not Moses and the prophets, neither will they be persuaded, though one rose from the dead**.

> *1 Timothy 1:5-7* Now the end of the commandment is charity out of a pure heart, and of a good conscience, and of faith unfeigned: [6]From which some having swerved have turned aside unto vain jangling; [7]**Desiring to be teachers of the law; understanding neither what they say, nor whereof they affirm**.

It is a curious thing how the Bible can have so many warnings to beware of deceivers, wolves in sheep's clothing, and yet so many fail to heed them, fail to preach or teach about them. Deceivers abound and must come; God uses them to try our hearts. To understand the Bible, it must be approached *"believing all things that are written"* and must be adhered to, not being swayed by those that believe not.

Deuteronomy 13:1-4 If there arise among you a prophet, or a dreamer of dreams, and giveth thee a sign or a wonder, [2]And **the sign or the wonder come to pass**, whereof he spake unto thee, saying, **Let us go after other gods**, which thou hast not known, and let us serve them; [3]**Thou shalt not hearken unto the words of that prophet, or that dreamer of dreams**: for the LORD your God **proveth you**, to know whether ye love the LORD your God with all your heart and with all your soul. [4]Ye shall walk after the LORD your God, and fear him, and keep his commandments, and obey his voice, and ye shall serve him, and cleave unto him.

2 Peter 2:1-2 But there were false prophets also among the people, even as there shall be false teachers among you, who privily shall bring in damnable heresies, even denying the Lord that bought them, and bring upon themselves swift destruction. [2]And **many shall follow their pernicious ways**; by reason of whom the way of truth shall be evil spoken of.

1 Corinthians 11:18-19 For first of all, when ye come together in the church, I hear that there be divisions among you; and I partly believe it. [19]For **there must be also heresies among you, that they which are approved may be made manifest among you**.

2 Timothy 2:15 **Study** to shew thyself approved unto God,

Within the Church today many controversies exist; it is more divided than ever caused by a falling away from the truth due to an ignorance of and lack of desire toward the Scriptures. If you are unwilling to make the necessary sacrifices to direct your life toward the Lord your God, *to* diligently seek, and believe your creator then you can expect confusion and uncertainty. Diversity of opinions abound; the council of God's word has been added to and diminished from, supplanted by the preaching of philosophy and the sciences, *"falsely so-called:"*—theistic evolution, psychology, the social sciences, etc.

Colossians 2:8 **Beware lest any man spoil you through philosophy** and vain deceit, after the tradition of men, after the rudiments of the world, and not after Christ.

1 Timothy 6:20 O Timothy, keep that which is committed to thy trust, avoiding profane and vain babblings, and oppositions **of science falsely so called**:

It is impossible to avoid those who choose not to believe, that add and diminish from God's word, who would have you follow them rather than diligently study the Scriptures. Believing the Bible will bring their disdain, contempt, and derision; to believe the truth is heresy with them.

Acts 24:14 But this I confess unto thee, that after the way which they call heresy, so worship I the God of my fathers, **believing all things which are written in the law and in the prophets**:

The third precept to understanding the Bible is:

Believe all things which are written

Bad men or devils would not have written the Bible, for it condemns them and their works, good men or angels could not have written it, for in saying it was from God when it was but their own invention, they would have been guilty of falsehood, and thus could not have been good. The only remaining being who could have written it is God—its real author.

—John Flavel 1627-91,
English Clergy

THE CONSTRUCTION
OF THE SCRIPTURES

For the prophecy came not in old time by the will of man: but holy men of God spake as they were moved by the Holy Ghost.

—2 PETER 1:21

4) Revelation
5) Similitudes
6) Rightly Divide
7) Precept Upon Precept

I believe the Bible is to be understood and received in the plain and obvious meaning of its passages; for I cannot persuade myself that a book intended for the instruction and conversion of the whole world should cover its true meaning in any such mystery and doubt that none but critics and philosophers can discover it.

—Daniel Webster 1782~1852
American Orator & Statesmen

39

Revelation

Surely the Lord God will do nothing, but he revealeth his secret unto his servants the prophets.

—AMOS 3:7

There is one very important and oft-forgotten precept of the Scriptures: *"All Things Are Possible."*

Luke 1:37 For with God **nothing shall be impossible**.

God was not restricted in the design of his plan by anything other than his own purposes. It is not a question of what God could have done; God could have done anything. The question is what has he revealed to us, whether through creation or his word, concerning himself and what he has done. Speaking in condemnation of idols, the Lord said:

> *Isaiah 41:21-23* Produce your cause, saith the LORD; bring forth your strong reasons, saith the King of Jacob. [22]Let them bring them forth, and shew us what shall happen: **let them shew the former things, what they be, that we may consider them, and know the latter end of them; or declare us things for to come.** [23]**Shew the things that are to come hereafter**, that we may know that ye are gods:

Here in Isaiah, it is shown that the proof of the divine authorship of the Bible is in its revelations: in making known the past, explaining the present, and revealing the future. The Bible is a book of revelations. This precept, according to Amos 3:7, states God has chosen not to do anything without revealing it: revealing himself, his person, personality, power, and plans.

> *Amos 3:7* Surely the **Lord GOD will do nothing, but he revealeth his secret unto his servants the prophets**.

This is especially so in these last days when the greater part of all prophecy is unfolding before our eyes so that there can be no excuse for not seeing his hand in everything. Whether revealed through the tapestry of history, wonders of nature, or mysteries of science, the key to all revelations is the revelation of God's word.

> *Isaiah 42:9* Behold, the former things are come to pass, and new things do I declare: **before they spring forth I tell you of them**.

> *Isaiah 45:21* Tell ye, and bring them near; yea, **let them take counsel together: who hath declared this from ancient time? who hath told it from that time? have not I the** LORD? and there is no God else beside me; a just God and a Saviour; there is none beside me.

40

Isaiah 46:9-10 Remember the former things of old: for I am God, and there is none else; I am God, and there is none like me, **¹⁰Declaring the end from the beginning, and from ancient times the things that are not yet done,**

One clarification that must be made regarding this precept. God does not prognosticate; he does not predict the future nor divine what shall come. God knows the future as he is in control of it. God controls events and guides them to the conclusions of his choice, his making. If he says a nation shall rise, he raises up that nation, etc. However, do not go over the deep end, as some have, in concluding all things predestinated, or all things being foreknown, that is not so. Much of the course of history has been God's judgments in response to man's actions as well as the thoughts and intents of the heart. The correct interpretation of the biblical flow of events is more complicated than the simplistic teachings that have prevailed in mainstream thinking. This will be expanded on in later chapters.

There is an underlying framework in God's plan containing all the major events of history: creation; the bringing forth the nation of Israel as a witness to the world; the raising up of the nations of Babylon; Medo-Persia, Greece; Rome; the Lord Jesus Christ and his first and second comings; the latter judgments and much more. Between these, however, is plenty of room for cause and effect as well as time and chance. Every nation in the world is not referred to in Scripture, but everyone is judged and dealt with following the examples God has set forth. It is often remarkably difficult to get some to understand and accept this; not understanding it limits the comprehension of God's word.

Ecclesiastes 7:29 Lo, this only have I found, that God hath made man upright; but **they have sought out many inventions**.

Ecclesiastes 9:11 I returned, and saw under the sun, that the race is not to the swift, nor the battle to the strong, neither yet bread to the wise, nor yet riches to men of understanding, nor yet favour to men of skill; but **time and chance happeneth to them all**.

The Bible being God's revelation of himself is the revelation of the Lord Jesus Christ.

Revelation 19:10 for the testimony of Jesus is **the spirit of prophecy**.

John 5:39 Search the scriptures; for in them ye think ye have eternal life: and **they are they which testify of me**.

Psalm 40:7 Then said I, Lo, I come: **in the volume of the book it is written of me**,

The mysteries of the Church and its doctrines and precepts are also made known by the revelations of the New Testament, not by philosophy or reason.

Galatians 1:12 For I neither received it of man, neither was I taught it, but **by the revelation of Jesus Christ**.

Ephesians 3:1-6 For this cause I Paul, the prisoner of Jesus Christ for you Gentiles, ²If ye have heard of the dispensation of the grace of God which is given me to you-ward: ³How that **by revelation** he made known unto me the mystery;... ⁵Which in other ages was not made known unto the sons of men, as it is **now revealed unto his holy apostles and prophets by the Spirit**; ⁶That the Gentiles should be fellowheirs, and of the same body, and partakers of his promise in Christ by the gospel:

This precept will become especially viable in relation to the next, that of similitudes; they are a major form of presenting the revelations in Scripture.

Personal knowledge of and relationship with God is through the revelation of his word. Creation manifests the existence and power of God, but to know him he must personally reveal himself through his word.

Psalm 19:1 **The heavens declare the glory of God; and the firmament sheweth his handywork.**

Isaiah 55:8 For **my thoughts are not your thoughts, neither are your ways my ways**, saith the LORD.

1 Samuel 3:7 Now Samuel did not yet know the LORD, **neither was the word of the LORD yet revealed unto him.**

It should be stressed at this point that these seven precepts are an inseparable unit; all interpretations of Scripture must conform to the whole of the fundamentals embodied in them. If faithful adherence to the first three precepts is maintained: to diligently study without adding nor diminishing from the Scriptures and believing all things that are written, the last four principles will follow quite naturally. The revelations of Scripture establish God's and the Bible's authenticity in explaining the past, giving understanding of the present, and revealing the future.

The fourth precept to understanding the Bible is:

It is God's Revelation

The biblical record is far more concerned with events than it is with ideas. Ideas there are, but they are subordinated to events. The conviction, usually unstated, is that God reveals himself much more fully in history than in nature or in any other way. The men who wrote the words of the Bible were contented, for the most part, with telling a story.

Elton Trueblood (1900-1994),
American Quaker and philosopher

Similitudes

I have also spoken by the prophets, and I have multiplied visions, and used similitudes, by the ministry of the prophets.

—Hosea 12:10

What would education be without the use of examples? Instruction in any craft or skill is based on learning the governing principles and studying examples of both the correct and incorrect, following these comes their application. It is the same with God's word. The Bible is a book of precepts and instruction by example or similitudes.

That the historical events recorded in the Scriptures are similitudes is of extreme importance to remember. The Bible was not written for the sole purpose of providing us with a historical record of the past, although its record is true. The segments of history that are recorded were done so for the express purpose of revelation. They are for revealing God, as described in precept 4, but just as importantly, there are examples of the personalities and characters of men.

Additionally, many of the historical accounts are graphic representations of spiritual events. As similitudes, the Scriptures transcend all historical and cultural limitations; the commandments, doctrines, and lessons of the Bible are eternal, as applicable today as when they were written. Its teachings cannot be dismissed on the tenuous excuse of historical progress or cultural bias. The times and cultures for the settings of the lessons of scripture were well chosen by God conveying his exact meaning. These teachings stand at any time in history; man has not evolved to greater truths or cultural advancements but has fallen away from the truth.

2 Timothy 3:16 **All scripture is given by inspiration of God**, and is profitable for doctrine, for reproof, for correction, for instruction in righteousness:

2 Peter 2:6 And turning the cities of Sodom and Gomorrha into ashes condemned them with an overthrow, **making them an ensample** unto those that after should live ungodly;

Jude 1:7 Even as Sodom and Gomorrha, and the cities about them in like manner, giving themselves over to fornication, and going after strange flesh, **are set forth for an example**,

Luke 17:26-30 And **as it was in the days of Noe**, so shall it be also in the days of the Son of man. ...[28]Likewise also **as it was in the days of Lot**; ...[30]Even **thus shall it be** in the day when the Son of man is revealed

Romans 15:4 For whatsoever things were written aforetime **were written for our learning**, that we through patience and comfort of the scriptures might have hope.

Romans 5:14 Nevertheless death reigned from Adam to Moses, even over them that had not sinned after the similitude of Adam's transgression, **who is the figure of him that was to come**.

Colossians 2:16-17 Let no man therefore judge you in meat, or in drink, or in respect of an holyday, or of the new moon, or of the sabbath days: [17]**Which are a shadow of things to come**; ...

Hebrews 4:11 Let us labour therefore to enter into that rest, lest any man fall after the same **example of unbelief**.

Hebrews 8:5 Who serve unto **the example and shadow of heavenly things**, as Moses was admonished of God when he was about to make the tabernacle: ...

1 Corinthians 10:11 Now all these things happened unto them for **ensamples**: and they are written for **our admonition**, upon whom the ends of the world are come.

Several similitudes are pointed out with explanations as to their interpretations giving us a guide to understanding and interpreting the others. An example to demonstrate the breadth and scope of this precept begins with allowing an ox to eat as it works and ends with its application to men.

Deuteronomy 25:4 **Thou shalt not muzzle the ox when he treadeth out the corn**.

1 Corinthians 9:9-10 For it is written in the law of Moses, **Thou shalt not muzzle the mouth of the ox that treadeth out the corn**. Doth God take care for oxen? [10]**Or saith he it altogether for our sakes? For our sakes**, no doubt, this is written: that he that ploweth should plow in hope; and that he that thresheth in hope should be partaker of his hope.

1 Timothy 5:17-18 Let the elders that rule well be counted worthy of double honour, especially they **who labour in the word and doctrine**. [18]For the scripture saith, **Thou shalt not muzzle the ox that treadeth out the corn**. And, **The labourer is worthy of his reward.**

Similitudes can come in a variety of forms, which will be briefly defined here. Probably every form of English style is represented within the Scriptures and you need to have some familiarity with them. Let us review the definition of similitude:

likeness; resemblance; likeness in nature, qualities, or appearance; comparison, simile, a representation; a facsimile; a portrait, allegory

James 3:9 Therewith bless we God, even the Father; and therewith curse we men, which are made after **the similitude** of God.

Biblical similitudes are represented in the follows forms:

1. **Allegory**—a symbolic representation

   Galatians 4:22-24 For it is written, that Abraham had two sons, the one by a bondmaid, the other by a freewoman. [23]But he who was of the bondwoman was born after the flesh; but he of the freewoman was by promise. [24]**Which things are an allegory**: for these are the two covenants; the one from the mount Sinai, which gendereth to bondage, which is Agar.

2. **Metaphor**—speaking of one object as if it were another

   - Sleep, the peaceable death of the saved.

     John 11:11-13 Our friend Lazarus sleepeth; but I go, that I may awake him out of sleep .... [13]Howbeit Jesus spake of his death:

     1 Thessalonians 4:14 For if we believe that Jesus died and rose again, even so them also **which sleep in Jesus** will God bring with him.

   - Light for truth and righteousness, Darkness for lies and unrighteousness.

     John 3:19 And this is the condemnation, that light is come into the world, and men loved **darkness rather than light**, because their deeds were evil.

   - The strait gate and narrow way of life opposed to the wide gate and broad way of death.

     Matthew 7:13 Enter ye in **at the strait gate**: for **wide is the gate**, and **broad is the way**, that leadeth to destruction, and many there be which go in thereat.

3. **Parable**—instruction not only in morals but in general knowledge made by comparison with natural or plain things. In the Scriptures, they are to give understanding in the things that pertain to God and his ways. Parables are also to hide the truth from those who do not follow our first three precepts.

   Matthew 13:10-11 And the disciples came, and said unto him, Why speakest thou unto them in parables? [11]He answered and said unto them, Because **it is given unto you to know** the mysteries of the kingdom of heaven, but **to them it is not given**.

4. **Paradigm**—a list, an example, serving as a model; pattern; A framework containing the basic assumptions, ways of thinking, and methodology. (Not all lists would constitute a paradigm.)

Proverbs 6:16-19 These six things doth the LORD hate: yea, **seven are an abomination unto him**:

- A proud look,
- A lying tongue,
- Hands that shed innocent blood
- An heart that deviseth wicked imaginations,
- Feet that be swift in running to mischief,
- A false witness that speaketh lies,
- He that soweth discord among brethren.

Paradigms can be descriptive lists of the constituent parts, rules, teachings, or behavior of individuals, organizations, or religious beliefs that recur throughout history. They may appear under different names or guises, and it is important to recognize and evaluate them correctly. The parts may not necessarily be contained in the same verse.

Matthew 6:7 But when ye pray, **use not vain repetitions, as the heathen do**: for they think that they shall be heard for their much speaking.

Matthew 23:9 And **call no man your father upon the earth**: for one is your Father, which is in heaven.

Mark 12:38 And he said unto them in his doctrine, Beware of the scribes, **which love to go in long clothing, and love salutations in the marketplaces,**

Luke 20:46-47 Beware of the scribes, **which desire to walk in long robes, and love greetings in the markets, and the highest seats in the synagogues**, and the **chief rooms at feasts; ⁴⁷Which devour widows' houses, and for a shew make long prayers**: the same shall receive greater damnation.

In the above verses, there are several descriptions of practices and mentalities given that transcend time and appear under different guises in history. When these descriptive acts are combined in a list, they form the system's constituent parts, a paradigm. The Lord specifically points these things out to be recognizable wherever or under what name they occur. The paradigm would be:

$X =$ Repetitious prayer
$=$ Religious titles e.g., Father
$=$ Long robes, i.e., religious costumes
$=$ Love of preeminence
$=$ Requires donations/payment for prayer and/or spiritual services

Many such lists are contained within the Scriptures. The Ten Commandments as a list is a paradigm, a set of conditions setting the proper parameters of life. Upon salvation one encounters a paradigm shift. You operate under a different list of conventions than when lost.

5. **Proverb**—a pithy saying condensing the wisdom of experience (e.g., the book of Proverbs)

6. **Simile**—a comparison or likeness using the words "like" or "as," etc.

> *Matthew 11:15-19* He that hath ears to hear, let him hear. [16]But **whereunto shall I liken this generation? It is like** unto children sitting in the markets, and calling unto their fellows, [17]And saying, **We have piped unto you, and ye have not danced; we have mourned unto you, and ye have not lamented.** [18]For John came neither eating nor drinking, and they say, He hath a devil. [19]The Son of man came eating and drinking, and they say, Behold a man gluttonous, and a winebibber, a friend of publicans and sinner.

> *Jeremiah 6:2* **I have likened** the daughter of Zion to a comely and delicate woman.

7. **Types**—descriptions or pictures God has woven into history

Remember our fourth precept, "Revelation," and examine Genesis chapter twenty-four for the types, similitudes, or pictures that God has woven into the fabric history.

> *Genesis 24:2-4* And Abraham said unto his eldest servant of his house, that ruled over all that he had, Put, I pray thee, thy hand under my thigh: And I will make thee swear by the LORD, the God of heaven, and the God of the earth, that thou shalt not take a wife unto my son of the daughters of the Canaanites, among whom I dwell: But **thou shalt go unto my country, and to my kindred, and take a wife unto my son Isaac.**

There are four main characters in the account: Abraham, Abraham's son Isaac, Abraham's unnamed servant, and Rebekah. In the narrative, Abraham sends his servant to his brethren to find a wife for his son. Everything needed to be known about Isaac's marriage can be summed up in one sentence: Isaac married Rebekah, the daughter of Bethuel the son of Milcah, the son of Nahor, Abraham's brother. That one sentence explains the genealogy of the family line. Yet, it is a lengthy chapter providing unessential detail of the event; what is the reason? The reason is that it is a similitude woven into history as a type of what is coming. The story is a prophecy of what God is doing and going to do.

The types are these:

1. Abraham = God the Father

2. Isaac = Christ Jesus

3. Servant = Holy Spirit

4. Rebekah = the Church, the bride of Christ

Abraham (God) sends his servant (Spirit) into the word to seek a wife for his son (Jesus). There are a few points to ponder in this.

- All that the Father has is given to the son:

    Genesis 24:35-36 And the LORD hath blessed my master greatly; and he is become great: and he hath given him flocks, and herds, and silver, and gold, and menservants, and maidservants, and camels, and asses. ... **unto him hath he given all that he hath**.

    Matthew 28:18 And Jesus came and spake unto them, saying, **All power is given unto me in heaven and in earth**.

    John 3:35 The Father loveth the Son, and **hath given all things into his hand**.

    John 5:22 For the Father judgeth no man, but **hath committed all judgment unto the Son**:

- The servant (Spirit) does not speak of himself but of the father and the son. The Holy Spirit does not speak of himself.

    John 16:13 Howbeit when he, the Spirit of truth, is come, he will guide you into all truth: for **he shall not speak of himself**; but whatsoever he shall hear, that shall he speak: and he will shew you things to come.

    Genesis 24:12 And he said, O LORD God of **my master Abraham**, I pray thee, send me good speed this day, and shew kindness unto **my master Abraham**.

    Genesis 24:27 And he said, Blessed be the LORD God of **my master Abraham**, who hath not left destitute **my master** of his mercy and his truth: I being in the way, the LORD led me to the house of **my master's** brethren.

    Genesis 24:49 And now if ye will deal kindly and truly with **my master**, tell me: and if not, tell me; that I may turn to the right hand, or to the left.

- Rebekah (Church) believes the witness of the servant (Spirit) and by faith accepts it.

    Genesis 24:58 And they called Rebekah, and said unto her, Wilt thou go with this man? And she said, **I will go**.

With diligent study a substantial amount of prophetic detail can be found in the historical stories of the Bible.

Many such types open the Scriptures as part of the revelations of our fourth precept. They graphically describe the operational methods, person, personality, and character of God, as well as that of men and Satan.

Marriage is one such type being a picture of the Church's relationship to our Lord.

> *Ephesians 5:31-32* For this cause shall a man leave his father and mother, and shall be joined unto his wife, and they two shall be one flesh. [32]This is a great mystery: but **I speak concerning Christ and the church**.

This is one reason marriage is constantly being assailed to destroy the picture and pattern in the minds of men of God's relationship with the Church. An epic work on the subject of similitudes is that of Preaching from the Types and Metaphors of the Bible.[3]

The fifth precept to understanding the Bible is:

God uses Similitudes

> The scriptures teach us the best way of living, the noblest way of suffering and the most comfortable way of dying.
>
> —John Flavel 1627-1691
> English Clergy

---

[3] Benjamin Keach (1640-1704) Kregel Publications, ISBN 0-8254-3008-9

Rightly Divide

Study to shew thyself approved unto God, a workman that needeth not to be ashamed, rightly dividing the word of truth.

—2 TIMOTHY 2:15

"Study to shew thyself approved unto God." The first thing noted is that to study is a command, an injunction, not a request nor a suggestion: study. A goal is given, a purpose for this study, that God's word might be rightly divided; in so doing the approval of God is obtained while failing to do so will bring shame before him. The obvious conclusion that must be drawn from this injunction is that to comprehend the Scriptures their proper divisions must be recognized and maintained, failing to rightly divide leads to misunderstanding and incorrect doctrinal teachings.

A correct understanding is not obtained easily, but through diligent study, *"labor in the word and doctrine."*

> *1 Timothy 5:17* Let the elders that rule well be counted worthy of double honour, especially they who **labour in the word and doctrine**.

> *1 Corinthians 3:8* …and every man shall receive his own reward **according to his own labour**.

The precept of rightly dividing will be found to be one of the major places where men fail in their efforts to correctly understand and interpret the Scriptures. Where the body of Christ wrongly divides the word of truth—it divides itself.

One division that must be made is determining who is being spoken to or about; the Jew, the Gentiles, or the Church.

> *1 Corinthians 10:32* Give none offence, neither to the **Jews**, nor to the **Gentiles**, nor to the **church** of **God**:

There are several books written on the topic of rightly dividing, which cover it in greater detail; here, the necessity of understanding it is pointed out. The following examples will demonstrate this necessity and complexity of rightly dividing the word of truth.

Example 1:

> *Isaiah 2:4* And he shall judge among the nations, and shall rebuke many people: and **they shall beat their swords into plow-shares, and their spears into pruninghooks**: nation shall not lift up sword against nation, neither shall they learn war any more.

Micah 4:3 And he shall judge among many people, and rebuke strong nations afar off; and **they shall beat their swords into plowshares, and their spears into pruninghooks**: nation shall not lift up a sword against nation, neither shall they learn war any more.

Verses

Joel 3:9-10 Proclaim ye this among the Gentiles; Prepare war, wake up the mighty men, let all the men of war draw near; let them come up: [10]**Beat your plowshares into swords, and your pruninghooks into spears**: let the weak say, I am strong.

The above two passages of Scripture advocate diametrically opposing commands; having a plowshare when a sword is needed or vice versa could be detrimental. In such a case, it must either be accepted that the Bible contradicts itself or there is a definite need to rightly divide the word of truth along historical lines. During the millennial reign of Christ, there will be no need for swords and spears, but until then, there shall be wars and rumors of wars.

Example 2:

Luke 4:16-21 This day is **this scripture fulfilled** in your ears.

The Lord in this passage is quoting Isaiah 61:1-3, but he stops halfway through, at a comma, and states that this prophecy is fulfilled by him at that time. Here is the whole passage separated where the Lord made the division:

Isaiah 61:1-3 The Spirit of the Lord GOD is upon me; because the LORD hath anointed me to preach **good tidings unto the meek**; he hath sent me **to bind up the brokenhearted**, to **proclaim liberty to the captives**, and the **opening of the prison to them that are bound**; [2]To **proclaim the acceptable year of the LORD,**

And then the prophecy continues:

and **the day of vengeance of our God**; to comfort all that mourn; [3]To appoint unto them that mourn in Zion, to give unto them beauty for ashes, the oil of joy for mourning, the garment of praise for the spirit of heaviness; that they might be called trees of righteousness, the planting of the LORD, that he might be glorified.

The division is between the first and second coming of our Lord. His first coming to proclaim salvation, his second when he returns to bring judgment upon the earth.

Notice that the division does not come at a verse break. The verse numbering system aids in finding and memorizing passages of Scripture but has no grammatical significance; the numbering does not affect meaning in any way. The Bible needs to be studied sentence by sentence. Remember, the smallest unit with definite meaning in grammar is the sentence. Errors are made simply due to breaking sentences at verse numberings and not maintaining the sentence structure. Dividing at verse numbers is wrongly dividing.

The verse numbers do serve an important function. Remember a sentence is a trinity: subject, predicate (verb), and a complete thought. It may, however, make its complete thought out of several sub-thoughts. The verse numbers divide the Bible into individual sub-thoughts. Here in 2 Corinthians, we have one sentence with three sub-thoughts making up the complete thought.

2 Corinthians 3:4-6

[4]And such trust have we through Christ to God-ward:

[5]Not that we are sufficient of ourselves to think any thing as of ourselves; but our sufficiency is of God;

[6]Who also hath made us able ministers of the new testament; not of the letter, but of the spirit: for the letter killeth, but the spirit giveth life.

We trust in God, who is all we need, making us able ministers of the New Testament which is not of the works of the law but the spirit of the law.

From the above two examples, it is seen that divisions must be made along the historical timeline; where in history do the components of prophecies properly belong? Many people in conversation have expressed that they are awaiting the great Gog and Magog battle setting the scene for this by describing current world events. Some become quite flabbergasted when informed they have at least a thousand years to wait according to the Bible.

Revelation 20: 7-8 And **when the thousand years are expired,** Satan shall be loosed out of his prison, [8]And shall go out to deceive the nations which are in the four quarters of the earth, **Gog and Magog, to gather them together to battle**: the number of whom is as the sand of the sea.

The great Gog-Magog battle does not take place until the end of the thousand-year reign of Christ.

Probably the most notable schism maker caused by not rightly dividing is the controversy between faith without works and faith and works as typified by the book of Romans verses James.

Romans 3:28 Therefore we conclude that a man is **justified by faith without the deeds of the law**.

James 2:24 Ye see then how that **by works a man is justified, and not by faith only**.

The mistake is in applying these two verses as speaking of the same thing; they are not. The cause for this is simply not diligently studying the passages. Divisions must be made; the Scriptures must be rightly divided. Other divisions must be made such as who is speaking and to whom: Jew, Gentiles, Church, or saved as opposed to the lost. Not all Scripture is directly applicable to the Church. One must always be careful of context when making divisions; as has been aptly stated, a text without a context is a pretext. In Romans, it is speaking of a person's individual eternal salvation, in James of demonstrating our faith once saved.

Hebrews 11:17 By faith Abraham, **when he was tried, offered up Isaac**: and he that had received the promises offered up his only begotten son,

James 2:20-23 But wilt thou know, O vain man, that **faith without works is dead**? [21]Was not Abraham our father **justified by works, when he had offered Isaac his son** upon the altar? [22]Seest thou how faith wrought with his works, and **by works was faith made perfect**? [23]And the scripture was fulfilled which saith, Abraham **believed God**, and **it was imputed unto him for righteousness**: and he was called the Friend of God.

Abraham's faith was proven by the trial God put him through. Your works are suppose to show the faith that saved you.

It is not faith and works;
It is not faith or works;
It is faith that works.

1 Peter 1:7 That **the trial of your faith**, being much more precious than of gold that perisheth, though it be tried with fire, might be found unto praise and honour and glory at the appearing of Jesus Christ:

Wrongly dividing the Scriptures is probably the cause of more errors in formulating incorrect doctrines than any other. Rightly dividing the Scriptures is impossible to do without diligent study, neither adding nor diminishing from the words, meaning, and context of its passages and having a proper believing attitude toward God's word. It cannot be emphasized enough that all Scripture must fit your doctrinal schemes or you have something wrong.

The last point in regard to this precept concerns the need to understand grammar. Many false teachings are based solely upon errors in reading caused by not understanding or applying basic grammar. When the Bible states, *"Study ... rightly dividing the word of truth,"* it isn't limiting that study to the word of truth only but anything required to be able to rightly divide it. Grammar is one of those things you must study. It is recommended that a refresher course in grammar be embarked upon for all serious students. You do not have to be an English major, just know and use the fundamentals.

The sixth precept to understanding the Bible is:

The word of truth must be
Rightly Divided

The word of God will stand a thousand readings; and he who has gone over it most frequently is the surest of finding new wonders there.

James Hamilton (1814-1867) English clergy-

Precept must be upon Precept

Whom shall he teach knowledge? and whom shall he make to understand doctrine? them that are weaned from the milk, and drawn from the breasts. For precept must be upon precept, precept upon precept; line upon line, line upon line; here a little, and there a little:

—ISAIAH 28:9-10

If carefully contemplated, the first six precepts of this study should provide ample evidence to recognize this principle in their construction, for it has been practiced throughout. We have been taking the word of God line upon line, a little here and a little there, and forming precepts. The precepts of the Bible are its universal inviolable general truths upon which all else is established. It is from these that correct doctrine must be built.

The preceding six precepts or general truths taken together, precept upon precept, establishes the doctrine of studying God's word. God's word must be diligently studied, it must not be added to nor diminished from, and all that is written must be believed, to be understood correctly. These three are the principles God requires of the heart. The Scriptures themselves are God's revelation of who he is and what he has done, is and will be doing, and what he requires. Further, the Bible teaches with similitudes, or examples, many times woven into history. Finally, it all must be rightly divided. These first six, all taken in conjunction, lead to the successful culmination of the seventh, establishing the correct doctrinal teachings based on the Bible's precepts. All the doctrines of Scripture must be built from the precepts contained therein.

Our title verse, Isaiah 28:9-13, explains the reason why the Bible is written the way it is, not only to teach knowledge and to give understanding in doctrine but to destroy those who refuse knowledge and understanding. *"That they might go, and fall backward, and be broken, and snared, and taken."*

The Bible, to those who will put their faith in God's word and diligently study it, neither adding nor diminishing from it and believing all that is written, is the source of knowledge and understanding in the things of God and this world.

Proverbs 2:1-6 My son, if thou wilt receive my words, and hide my commandments with thee; [2]So that thou incline thine ear unto wisdom, and apply thine heart to understanding; [3]Yea, **if thou criest after knowledge, and liftest up thy voice for understanding;** [4]**If thou seekest her as silver, and searchest for her as for hid treasures;** [5]**Then shalt thou understand the fear of the** LORD, **and find the knowledge of God.** [6]**For the** LORD

giveth wisdom: out of his mouth cometh knowledge and understanding.

To those who are not diligent, not believing, and who add and diminish from the words of the book, it is laden with snares to mislead and befuddle, refusing them knowledge and understanding, leaving them confused or caught in a lie.

Proverbs 1:20-33 Wisdom crieth with out; she uttereth her voice in the streets: [21]She crieth in the chief place of concourse, in the openings of the gates: in the city she uttereth her words, saying, [22]**How long, ye simple ones, will ye love simplicity? and the scorners delight in their scorning, and fools hate knowledge?** [23]Turn you at my reproof: behold, I will pour out my spirit unto you, I will make known my words unto you. [24]Because I have called, and ye refused; I have stretched out my hand, and no man regarded; [25]But **ye have set at naught all my counsel, and would none of my reproof:** [26]I also will laugh at your calamity; I will mock when your fear cometh; [27]When your fear cometh as desolation, and your destruction cometh as a whirlwind; when distress and anguish cometh upon you. [28]**Then shall they call upon me, but I will not answer; they shall seek me early, but they shall not find me:** [29]**For that they hated knowledge, and did not choose the fear of the** LORD: [30]They would none of my counsel: they despised all my reproof. [31]Therefore shall they eat of the fruit of their own way, and be filled with their own devices. [32]For the turning away of the simple shall slay them, and the prosperity of fools shall destroy them. [33]But **whoso hearkeneth unto me shall dwell safely, and shall be quiet from fear of evil.**

1 Corinthians 1:25-29 Because the foolishness of God is wiser than men; and the weakness of God is stronger than men. [26]For ye see your calling, brethren, how that **not many wise men after the flesh, not many mighty, not many noble, are called:** [27]**But God hath chosen the foolish things of the world to confound the wise; and God hath chosen the weak things of** the world to **confound the things which are mighty;** [28]**And base things of the world, and things which are despised, hath God chosen, yea, and things which are not, to bring to nought things that are:** [29]That **no flesh should glory in his presence.**

Who can receive this knowledge and understanding?

Isaiah 28:9 Whom shall he teach knowledge? and whom shall he make to understand doctrine? **them that are weaned from the milk, and drawn from the breasts.**

Hebrews 5:11-14 Of whom we have many things to say, and hard to be uttered, seeing ye are dull of hearing. [12]For when for the time ye ought to be teachers, **ye have need that one teach you again which be the first principles of the oracles of God;** and are become **such as have need of milk, and not of strong meat.** [13]For **every one that useth milk is unskilful in the word of righteousness: for he is a babe.** [14]But **strong meat belongeth to them that are of full age, even those who by reason of use have their senses exercised to discern both good and evil.**

Understanding is for those who are weaned from the milk and ready for the meat of the word. Our growth as Christians is required; spiritual growth and our understanding go hand in hand.

Hebrews 12:1 Wherefore seeing we also are compassed about with so great a cloud of witnesses, **let us lay aside every weight, and the sin which doth so easily beset us, and let us run with patience the race that is set before us,**

The doctrines of God are the facts concerning what he has established as the moral laws, standards, requirements, and responsibilities on any given subject according to the precepts of the Bible. The precepts are developed by studying and taking the relevant parts *"here a little, and there a little"* and putting them *"line upon line"* as these studies have attempted to demonstrate. No biblical doctrine or teaching can be correct if it violates any of God's precepts, general truths, upon which all else must be founded. Without a correct understanding of the Bible's doctrines the Church is what it has become—weak and divided. Without sound doctrine the Chruch is confusion.

1 Corinthians 14:33 For **God is not the author of confusion,**

Romans 16:17 Now I beseech you, brethren, mark them which cause divisions and offences **contrary to the doctrine which ye have learned;**

1 Timothy 4:6 If thou put the brethren in remembrance of these things, thou shalt be a good minister of Jesus Christ, nourished up in the **words of faith and of good doctrine**, whereunto thou hast attained.

1 Timothy 4:13-16 Till I come, give attendance to **reading, to exhortation, to doctrine.** ... [16]Take heed unto thyself, and unto the doctrine; continue in them: for in doing this thou shalt both **save thyself, and them that hear thee.**

1 Timothy 5:17 Let the elders that rule well be counted worthy of double honour, **especially they who labour in the word and doctrine.**

2 Timothy 4:2 Preach the word; be instant in season, out of season; reprove, rebuke, exhort with all longsuffering and **doctrine.**

2 Timothy 3:16 **All scripture** is given by inspiration of God, and **is profitable for doctrine**, for reproof, for correction, for instruction in righteousness:

In the absence of correct doctrine reproof, correction, and instruction, all would be in error.

> *Titus 1:9* Holding fast the faithful word as he hath been taught, that he may be able **by sound doctrine** both to exhort and to convince the gainsayers.

> *Titus 2:1* But speak thou the things which become **sound doctrine**:

> *Titus 2:7* In all things shewing thyself a pattern of good works: **in doctrine shewing uncorruptness**, gravity, sincerity,

Understanding the correct doctrinal teachings of the Scriptures is one of the main necessities in life.

> *2 Timothy 4:3-4* For **the time will come when they will not endure sound doctrine**; but after their own lusts shall they heap to themselves teachers, having itching ears; [4]And they shall turn away their ears from the truth, **and shall be turned unto fables**.

As part of studying the Scriptures, a list could and should be made of the biblical precepts as they are discovered. The biblical precepts are simply God's stated principles or the general truths on how he has determined and established all things, and no doctrine can be correct if it attempts to evade any one of them. You cannot formulate correct biblical doctrines without having an accurate understanding of the precepts upon which they are built. Any doctrinal statement or teaching that violates any biblical precept is in error.

The seventh precept to understanding the Bible is:

Doctrine must be built
Precept upon Precept,
line upon line,
here a little and there a little

Let the world progress as much as it likes; Let all branches of human research develop to the very utmost; nothing will take the place of the Bible.

Johann Wolfgang von Goethe (1749-1832)
German poet, playwright, novelist, scientist, statesman[4]

---

[4] Goethe was considered the greatest German literary figure of the modern era

SUMMARY

Study to shew thyself approved unto God, a workman that needeth not to be ashamed, rightly dividing the word of truth.

—*2 TIMOTHY 2:15*

The more I speak with people, the more I have felt that the lack of understanding these precepts and their recognition as an inseparable unit and guide has hindered many from having a greater comprehension of God's Holy Word. It is impossible to establish sound doctrine and correct teaching without adhering to these precepts. They act as a guide to meditation and, more importantly, limits the imagination, and bring order to the study of the Scriptures. It is hoped that this study has conveyed the need to recognize and consider these principles.

Whenever establishing doctrinal teachings or searching the Scriptures to judge the things that are said the following must be asked.

1) Is this the product of *diligent* study and not feigned words, philosophy, or private interpretation? Have all relevant passages been considered?

2) Has anything been *added to or diminished from* the words, sense, or understanding of the Bible?

3) Is all being *believed*? Is any part of the Bible being denied or disbelieved?

4) Anything is possible, but is this the truth God is *revealing*?

5) What are the *similitudes*, examples, or illustrations, given within the Scriptures concerning the subject or topic under consideration?

6) Are things *rightly divided*? Be sure you are not comparing apples with oranges.

7) Locate God's *precepts*. What are the guiding principles and limiting truths that apply?

It is only when conclusions drawn conform to all seven precepts that you can be assured of being on solid ground in establishing the doctrines of the Bible. God is the author of order, and these principles are the rules of order in studying and understanding his word.

In regard to this Great book, I have but to say, it is the best gift God has given to man. All the good the Savior gave to the world was communicated through this book. But for it, we could not know right from wrong. All things most desirable for man's welfare, here and hereafter, are to be found portrayed in it.

Abraham Lincoln (1809-1865)
16th President of United States

PRECEPTS

INTRODUCTION

**Thou hast commanded us
to keep thy precepts diligently**

—PSALMS 119:4

**For precept must be upon precept
precept upon precept;
line upon line, line upon line;
here a little, and there a little:**

—ISAIAH 28:10

In the previous study, we learned that to understand anything correctly you must learn and grasp the general principles or precepts that govern the processes of any given course. In Mathematics you must know the established conventions the order of operations and functions; in reading and writing, grammar: the set of structural rules governing the composition of clauses, phrases, and words in any given language. The study of science is the study of the general laws or principles that govern all things: the laws of motion, forces, energy, etc. Music has the laws of pipes and strings. The building trades have their fundamentals: carpentry, plumbing, roofing, etc. These precepts or general principles are the foundation of the processes involved and do not change regardless of the circumstance or situation. They are the lowest common denominators. The world conforms to these unchanging rules of behavior.

The following studies are an attempt to introduce the concept of studying the Bible *"precept upon precept."* To aid in understanding this method of learning the Bible, several biblical precepts are presented for your consideration. There is no order of importance in the listing, all are equally necessary to comprehend the Bible, some more easily explained and less debated than others. It is hoped that you will establish and be guided by the biblical precepts in your studies, *"line upon line, here a little, there a little,"* as required by the Scriptures. God is the author of order, and these principles are the rules of order in studying and understanding his word. Any teaching that violates any one of them is in error.

The Great Precepts

Jesus said unto him, Thou shalt love the Lord thy God with all thy heart, and with all thy soul, and with all thy mind. This is the first and great commandment. And the second is like unto it, Thou shalt love thy neighbour as thyself. On these two commandments hang all the law and the prophets.

—*MATTHEW 22:37-40*

There is none other commandment greater than these.

—*MARK 12:31*

The first two precepts of God's word are to *"love the Lord thy God with all thy heart, and with all thy soul, and with all thy mind,"* and to *"love thy neighbour as thyself."* On these two commandments hang the law and everything else.

Deuteronomy 6:5 And **thou shalt love the LORD thy God with all thine heart, and with all thy soul, and with all thy might**.

Joshua 23:11 Take good heed therefore unto yourselves, **that ye love the LORD your God**.

Romans 8:28 And we know that all things work together for good to them that **love God**, to them who are the called according to his purpose.

Leviticus 19:18 Thou shalt not avenge, nor bear any grudge against the children of thy people, but **thou shalt love thy neighbour as thyself:** I am the LORD.

Leviticus 19:34 But **the stranger** that dwelleth with you shall be unto you as one born among you, and thou **shalt love him as thyself**; for ye were strangers in the land of Egypt: I am the LORD your God.

Galatians 5:14 For all the law is fulfilled in one word, even in this; **Thou shalt love thy neighbour as thyself**.

James 2:8 If ye fulfil **the royal law** according to the scripture, **Thou shalt love thy neighbour as thyself**, ye do well:

As you can see these precepts are universal; Old or New Testament, they have always been and always will be the two Great Precepts of God and the fulfillment of his law. As you can also see, man tends to cut God out, making the second law, the Golden Rule, instead of loving God, it is to love your neighbor. Love your neighbor is the Royal Law, not the Golden Rule.

The first two precepts of God's word:

Love God with all your heart, mind, and soul
—the Golden Rule

Love your neighbor as your self
—the Royal Law

All Things are Possible

Yea, they turned back and tempted God, and limited the Holy One of Israel.

—PSALM 78:41

It has been my opinion, subsequent to having dealt with numerous individuals, that this very important precept is an oft-forgotten principle of the scriptures. I cannot tell you how many times I have been told that God could not have done something because it was impossible, or it would have tainted him in some way. We are not looking for what God could have done; God could have done anything. As the following verses testify, the Bible clearly teaches the precept that nothing is impossible for God. We are looking not for what he could have done, but for what he has revealed to us in the Scriptures concerning what he has done.

Matthew 19:26 But Jesus beheld them, and said unto them, With men this is impossible; but **with God all things are possible.**

Mark 10:27 And Jesus looking upon them saith, With men it is impossible, but not with God: for **with God all things are possible.**

Luke 1:37 For **with God nothing shall be Impossible.**

Luke 18:27 And he said, **The things which are Impossible with men are possible with God.**

Psalm 78:41 Yea, they turned back and tempted God, and **limited the Holy One of Israel,**

Jeremiah 32:27 Behold, I am the LORD, the God of all flesh: **is there any thing too hard for me?**

All things are possible for God nothing is impossible for him. God could have established salvation by works as easily as by faith. He could have established all things as taught by Islam, Buddhism, Hinduism, Catholicism, Mormonism, or any other. It is not a question of what God could have done; it is what has he revealed of his doings.

This precept can be an effective witness. Many times in dealing with a Jewish individual, I have ended all their arguments simply by asking them if there is anything impossible for God. They will inevitably answer no, nothing is impossible for God. At that response, I state, "Then God could have manifested himself in the flesh as his own son if he wanted to." To this, I will receive one of two responses: silent confused acquiescence to this truth or, they will yell, "Impossible, Impossible," and turn to speed away.

Precept:

With God all things are possible

Naked In, Naked Out

For we brought nothing into this world, and it is certain we can carry nothing out.

—I TIMOTHY 6:7

I often think of the Pharaohs and ancient Emperors of China when I think of this precept. How they buried everything to take with them, yet all their treasures remain with us. You can't take it with you. Unfortunately, many in this world act as if they can.

James 5:3 **Your gold and silver is cankered; and the rust of them shall be a** witness **against you**, and shall eat your flesh as it were fire. Ye have heaped treasure together for the last days.

We came into this world without any material possessions and we are leaving the same way.

Job 1:21 And said, **Naked came I out of my mother's womb, and naked shall I return thither**: the LORD gave, and the LORD hath taken away; blessed be the name of the LORD.

Psalm 49:17 For **when he dieth he shall carry nothing away**: **his glory shall not descend after him**.

Ecclesiastes 5:15 **As he came forth of his mother's womb, naked shall he return to go as he came**, and shall take **nothing of his labour, which he may carry away in his hand**.

1 Timothy 6:7 For **we brought nothing into this world**, and **It is certain we can carry nothing out**.

The rich of this world are a long way from the example of that perfect servant of the Lord, Job.

Job 29:12-16 Because I delivered the poor that cried, and the fatherless, and him that had none to help him. [13]The blessing of him that was ready to perish came upon me: and I caused the widow's heart to sing for joy. [14]I put on righteousness, and it clothed me: my judgment was as a robe and a diadem. [15]I was eyes to the blind, and feet was I to the lame. [16]I was a father to the poor: and the cause which I knew not I searched out.

It is not going with you; what you do with it here while it is in your power is how you will be judged.

Matthew 6:19-21 **Lay not up for yourselves treasures upon earth**, where moth and rust doth corrupt, and where thieves break through and steal: [20]But **lay up for yourselves treasures in heaven**, where neither moth nor rust doth corrupt, and where thieves do not break through nor steal: [21]For **where your treasure Is, there will your heart be** also.

1 Timothy 6:4-5 He is proud, knowing nothing, but doting about questions and strifes of words, ...⁵and destitute of the truth, **supposing that gain is godliness**: from such withdraw thyself.

The rich of this world are going to have a lot to answer for:

1 Samuel 2:7 The LORD **maketh poor**, and **maketh rich**: he **bringeth low**, and **lifteth up**.

Luke 12:48 For unto **whomsoever much is given, of him shall be much required**:

Precept:

**We brought nothing into this world,
and It is certain we can carry nothing out**

The Wrath of Man

Wherefore, my beloved brethren,
let every man be swift to hear,
slow to speak, slow to wrath:

—James 1:19

There is a short quick one verse universal precept of God's word condemning man's wrath, or as some would say our righteous indignation, toward that which we think offends God.

James 1:20 For **the wrath of man worketh not the righteousness of God**.

Our anger, righteous indignation, holy wrath, or whatever one might want to call it has no place in ministering the gospel of Jesus Christ or in serving God; man's wrath is in no way allowed by God in his service. This is supported throughout God's word.

Matthew 5:44 But I say unto you, **Love your enemies, bless them that curse you, do good to them that hate you**, and **pray for them which despitefully use you**, and **persecute you**;

Luke 6:28 **Bless them that curse you**, and **pray for them which despitefully use you**.

Romans 12:14 **Bless them which persecute you: bless, and curse not**.

2 Timothy 2:24-25 And the servant of the Lord **must not strive; but be gentle unto all men, apt to teach, patient,** [25]**In meekness** instructing those that oppose themselves;

This is a universal precept, not just for the ministry. Our wrath does not equate to serving God in any circumstance.

Precept:

The wrath of man
worketh not the righteousness of God

One Mediator

**For there is one God, and one mediator between
God and men, the man Christ Jesus;**

—*I TIMOTHY 2:5*

The Scriptures are quite adamant, there is only one mediator, one Saviour, one name under heaven that reconciles us to God.

Job 19:25 For **I know that my redeemer liveth**, and that he shall stand at the latter day upon the earth:

1 Timothy 2:5 For there is one God, and **one mediator** between God and men, **the man Christ Jesus**;

Hebrews 9:14-15 How much more shall the blood of Christ, who through the eternal Spirit offered himself without spot to God, purge your conscience from dead works to serve the living God? [15]And for this cause **he is the** mediator **of the new testament**, ...

Acts 4:12 **Neither is there salvation in any other**: for **there is none other name under heaven given** among men, **whereby we must be saved**.

1 John 5:12 **He that hath the Son hath life**; and **he that hath not the Son of God hath not life**.

John 3:18 He that believeth on him is not condemned: but he that believeth not is condemned already, **because he hath not believed in the name of the only begotten Son of God**.

The Bible leaves no room for "co-mediators" or "co-mediatrix's." Christ was not just a prophet, a good man; he is the Saviour, the only Saviour man has. The Scriptures leave no room for the concept that all or any other religion can lead to God and salvation. This is what the world, the lost, cannot abide; and therefore, as foretold, they deny the actual person of Jesus Christ, teaching the precepts and principles of a mythological character they neither trust nor believe in.

1 John 4:2-3 Hereby know ye the Spirit of God: **Every spirit that confesseth that Jesus Christ is come in the flesh is of God**: [3]And **every spirit that confesseth not** that Jesus Christ is come in the flesh **is not of God**: and this is that spirit of antichrist, whereof ye have heard that it should come; and even now already is it in the world.

2 John 1:7 For many deceivers are entered into the world, who **confess not** that Jesus Christ is come in the flesh. **This is a deceiver and an antichrist**.

Precept:

**For there is one God, and one mediator
between God and men, the man Christ Jesus**

Not of Works

And enter not into judgment with thy servant: for in thy sight shall no man living be justified.

—*Psalm 143:2*

Unfortunately, unlike some of the other precepts that enjoy almost universal appeal, this precept deals with a topic of some debate. Do our works have any part, or have works ever played a part in eternal salvation? I believe in this study, we will find the answer to be a firm no, establishing the fact as a universal precept of God's word.

Psalms 143:1-2 **in thy sight shall no man living be justified**.

The above verse alone ought to be enough to convince anyone: *"in thy sight shall no man living be justified."* How is it then that some say we must have works for salvation? That we can be justified before God in and of ourselves? The following verses relate specifically to this topic to form the biblical precept that salvation is never by works.

Romans 3:20 Therefore **by the deeds of the law there shall no flesh be justified** in his sight:

Galatians 3:21-22 Is the law then against the promises of God? God forbid: for **if there had been a law given which could have given life, verily righteousness should have been by the law**. [22]But the scripture hath concluded all under sin, that the promise by faith of Jesus Christ might be given to them that believe.

Galatians 2:16 **Knowing that a man is not justified by the works of the law**, but by the faith of Jesus Christ, even we have believed in Jesus Christ, that we might be justified by the faith of Christ, and **not by the works of the law**: for **by the works of the law shall no flesh be justified**.

Isaiah 64:6 But **we are all as an unclean thing, and all our righteousnesses are as filthy rags**; and we all do fade as a leaf; and our iniquities, like the wind, have taken us away.

It is evident that eternal salvation, biblically, certainly does not come by works alone, as many of the religions of the world teach. However, some still try to keep works in the equation by making it works and faith. The following passages of Scripture show that if there is an element of works involved, whether in obtaining salvation or maintaining it, then faith is made void and salvation is not by the grace of God.

Romans 4:4-5 Now **to him that worketh** is the reward **not reckoned of grace, but of debt**. [5]But **to him that worketh not, but believeth on him that justifieth the ungodly, his faith is counted for righteousness**.

Romans 4:14 For if they which are of the law be heirs, **faith is made void, and the promise made of none effect**:

Romans 11:6 And **if by grace, then is it no more of works**: otherwise grace is no more grace. But **if it be of works, then is it no more grace**: otherwise work is no more work.

If salvation is by the grace of God, then there can be no part of it by works, at all; faith and works are mutually exclusive. If you are given a free gift and then told you have to pay to keep it, grace and free went out the window; all that matters now is did you pay for it, or did you not pay. There is no grace involved. I am not thankful for a free gift; I am demanding what I paid for, *"Now to him that worketh is the reward not reckoned of grace, but of debt."*

Romans 4:16 Therefore **it is of faith, that it might be by grace**;

Ephesians 2:8-9 For **by grace are ye** saved **through faith**; and that **not of yourselves**: it is the gift of God: [9]**Not of works**, lest any man should boast.

We find grace in God's eyes when we believe him, his word, his revelation of himself. When we believe his account of how he hung his Son, Jesus Christ, on a tree and made him a curse for us. It is according to his grace that he applies the shed blood of the Lord's atonement to our sins. God will have no man stand before him and boast his own righteousness.

These verses establish a universal biblical precept, not just a church age or dispensational teaching. Eternal salvation is never by works, alone or in concert with faith. Any teaching to the contrary is not biblical, not Christian doctrine. Unless this precept is accepted you will error in the formation of other doctrines.

Job 25:4-6 **How then can man be justified with God**? or **how can he be clean that is born of a woman**? [5]Behold even to the moon, and it shineth not; yea, the stars are not pure in his sight. [6]**How much less man, that is a worm**? and **the son of man, which is a worm**?

Job 19:25 For **I know that my** redeemer **liveth**, and that he shall stand at the latter day upon the earth:

Precept:

Salvation is not conditioned on man's works

All Men

The LORD taketh pleasure in them that fear him, in those that hope in his mercy.

—*PSALM 147:11*

In this precept, we shall see that all men were created equal, at least in so far as salvation is concerned. All were created to fear God and hope in his mercy and have the same opportunity to be saved.

Revelation 4:11 Thou art worthy, O Lord, to receive glory and honour and power: for thou hast created all things, and **for thy pleasure they are and were created**.

Ezekiel 33:11 Say unto them, As I live, saith the Lord GOD, **I have no pleasure in the death of the wicked; but that the wicked turn from his way and live**: turn ye, turn ye from your evil ways; for why will ye die, O house of Israel?

Ezekiel 18:23 **Have I any pleasure at all that the wicked should die**? saith the Lord GOD: **and not that he should return from his ways, and live**?

Ezekiel 18:32 For **I have no pleasure in the death of him that dieth**, saith the Lord GOD: wherefore **turn yourselves, and live ye**.

If God created all things for his pleasure and takes no pleasure in the death of the wicked, then he created all men to be pleasing to him. He did not create anyone to be wicked, to go to hell, or without the same opportunity as everyone else to seek him and be pleasing to him. If God takes no pleasure in the wicked and all things were created for his pleasure, then what did he create man for?

Psalms 147:11 The LORD **taketh pleasure in them that fear him, in those that hope in his mercy**.

Precept:

**God created all men
to fear him and hope in his mercy**

Whosoever

For God so loved the world, that he gave his only begotten Son, that whosoever believeth in him should not perish, but have everlasting life.

—<small>JOHN</small> 3:16

The LORD taketh pleasure in them that fear him, in those that hope in his mercy.

—<small>PSALM</small> 147:11

John 3:16 is probably the most famous verse in the Bible; it is the most famous of the *"whosoever"* verses. The word "whosoever" appears sixty-six times in the Bible and yet some deny this greatest of precepts; salvation is to *"whosoever believeth,"* and *"whosoever will not"* is blotted out of the book of life. It has always been whosoever will or whosoever will not.

> *Exodus 32:33* And the LORD said unto Moses, **Whosoever hath sinned** against me, **him will I blot out of my book**.

> *Deuteronomy 18:19* And it shall come to pass, that **whosoever will not hearken unto my words** which he shall speak in my name, **I will require it of him**.

> *Matthew 10:32-33* **Whosoever** therefore **shall confess me** before men, him will I confess also before my Father which is in heaven. [33]But **whosoever shall deny me** before men, him will I also deny before my Father which is in heaven.

We can also put a finer point on the definition of *"whosoever."*

> *John 3:16* For God so loved **the world**, that he gave his only begotten Son, **that whosoever believeth in him** should not perish, but have everlasting life.

What set or group, subset or subgroup of people is being spoken of here? It is the group of people consisting of the world, *"God so loved the world."* It is not a subgroup of a limited elect or any other lesser set of people. It is *"whosoever believeth"* out of the whole *"world."* This includes the entire human race.

It must also be remembered from the preceding precept; God created all things for his pleasure and the ramifications of that. If God created all things for his pleasure and takes no pleasure in the death of the wicked, then he did not create any man to die the death of the wicked but for all to be pleasing to him.

> *Psalms 147:11* The LORD **taketh pleasure in them that fear him, in those that hope in his mercy**.

God takes no pleasure in the death of the wicked but does in the wicked turning from his wicked ways and joining those that fear him, in those that hope in his mercy. How can any doctrine or teaching be correct if it rejects this precept?

Many pervert the clear teaching of Scripture, blinded to it for whatever reason, and teach other false interpretations. An example of this is Romans chapter nine. They take a couple of verses out of the chapter and preach predestination while the context of the whole chapter teaches *"whosoever will,"* as plainly stated in the last verse.

> *Romans 9:33* As it is written, Behold, I lay in Sion a stumbling-stone and rock of offence: and **whosoever believeth on him** shall not be ashamed.

It is man's free choice whether he is one of those that belong to whosoever will or whosoever will not.

Precept:

It is whosoever will out of all men

It should be seen how the last four precepts combine to form a greater understanding of God's doctrine of salvation: One Mediator, All Men, Whosoever, Not of Works.

Once Saved

And grieve not the holy Spirit of God, whereby ye are sealed unto the day of redemption.

—Ephesians 4:30

John 6:37-40 All that the Father giveth me shall come to me; and him that cometh to me **I will in no wise cast out**. [38]For I came down from heaven, not to do mine own will, but the will of him that sent me. [39]And **this is the Father's will** which hath sent me, that of all which he hath given me **I should lose nothing**, but should raise it up again at the last day. [40]And **this is the will of him that sent me**, that every one which seeth the Son, and believeth on him, **may have everlasting life**: and I will raise him up at the last day.

Those who teach the loss of salvation do greatly error not knowing the Scriptures. Salvation is not by our works. Salvation is not obtained nor maintained by self-righteousness, keeping the law.

Romans 11:6 And **if by grace, then is it no more of works**: … **if it be of works, then is it no more grace**:

Romans 4:4 Now to him that worketh is the reward not reckoned of grace, **but of debt**.

Ephesians 2:8 For **by grace are ye saved through faith**; and that **not of yourselves**: it is the gift of God: [9]**Not of works**, lest any man should boast.

Romans 5:18 Therefore as by the offence of one judgment came upon all men to condemnation; even so by the righteousness of one **the free gift** came upon all men unto justification of life.

If you received the free gift of grace and find a payment book attached, what happens to grace, free, and gift? They are expelled; grace and works are mutually exclusive. It is by grace or by works there is no grace and works. You did not work to get your salvation nor is it maintained by works, as the Galatians errored in thinking.

Galatians 3:2-3 This only would I learn of you, **Received ye the Spirit by the works of the law, or by the hearing of faith**? [3]Are ye so foolish? **having begun in the Spirit, are ye now made perfect by the flesh**?

The security of the believer is our liberty in Christ.

Hebrews 2:15 And deliver them who through fear of death were **all their lifetime subject to bondage**.

If salvation could be lost, the saints would still be in bondage to the law and fearful of death.

Galatians 2:4 And that because of **false brethren** unawares brought in, who came in privily to spy out **our liberty which we have in Christ Jesus**, that **they might bring us into bondage**:

The erroneous idea is set forth that Judas lost his salvation. Not only was Judas not ever saved, no one could be saved until after Christ made the atonement. Judas was dead before then.[5] If you can lose your salvation by not maintaining good works then salvation is by works.

Galatians 5:4 Christ is become of no effect unto you, whosoever of you are justified by the law; **ye are fallen from grace**.

Galatians 2:21 I do not frustrate the grace of God: for **if righteousness come by the law, then Christ is dead in vain**.

Galatians 3:21 Is the law then against the promises of God? God forbid: for **if there had been a law given which could have given life**, verily righteousness should have been by the law.

Romans 10:3-4 For they being ignorant of God's righteousness, and going about to establish their own righteousness, have not submitted themselves unto the righteousness of God. [4]For **Christ is the end of the law for righteousness to every one that believeth**.

We were created unto good works, but not saved by them.

These examples should suffice in demonstrating that we must maintain the precepts of the Bible to correctly interpret the doctrines of Scripture, doctrine must be built precept upon precept. Seek out the precepts of God's word, as we now will attempt to do, and the doctrines will fall into place.

---

[5]See the chapter: Salvation; and subchapter: Dispensational Salvation.

SALVATION

METHODOLOGY OF SALVATION

**For precept must be upon precept, precept
upon precept;
line upon line, line upon line;
here a little, and there a little:**

—*ISAIAH 28:10*

When it comes to the doctrine of Eternal Salvation, as with most doctrines, there is much disagreement on its proper interpretation. Naturally, the methodology of salvation is under attack from all sides. What is the correct form or methodology of this most important doctrine? This study looks at the biblical precepts that guide our understanding and limit our imagination as to how our salvation was accomplished.

Many are not aware of the amount of disputing and contention that there is concerning this doctrine. Does man have free will or is he predestinated? Is he required to have faith, or is he given faith? Do our works play any part in our salvation? Does one have to be a member of a particular denomination or church? Is baptism necessary for salvation? The disputes are endless and to our shame.

To understand this doctrine, we must first consider the precepts or general principles that govern it. In the chapter Precepts of the Bible several precepts that were directly related to salvation were given as examples. One answered the question is salvation in whole or in part dependent upon our works? This was easy to comprehend as we were given the answer in no uncertain terms; there was very little to interpret.

> *Romans 11:6* And **if by grace, then is it no more of works**: otherwise grace is no more grace. But **if it be of works, then is it no more grace**: otherwise work is no more work.

> *Romans 4:16* Therefore **it is of faith, that it might be by grace**;

> *Ephesians 2:5* Even when we were dead in sins, hath quickened us together with Christ, (**by grace ye are saved**;)

It is not known at the time of this writing if there is any sect or denomination claiming to be Christian that does not hold to salvation being wholly or in part God's grace? What the Bible explains, that many fail to understand, is that grace and works are mutually exclusive of each other. If eternal salvation is by the grace of God, then there can be no part of it by works; *"if by grace, then is it no more of works."* The two, grace and works, are mutually exclusive.

If I say to my son, "Son, you have found grace in my sight. Therefore, I am going to let you use the car tonight, if you mow the lawn." With the inclusion of the works, grace went out the window. All that matters now is did my son mow the lawn, or did he not? There is no grace involved; he either cut the grass or he did not. This may be a simplistic example, but it is an accurate one. My son is not coming to me thanking me for my mercy and grace, he is demanding what I owe him for the work he did.

Romans 4:4 Now to him that worketh **is the reward not reckoned of grace, but of debt.**

Many persist, nevertheless, in teaching as Bible truth that an element of works is required in obtaining or maintaining salvation. Both teachings were the subject of the great counsel and debate of Acts chapter 15 and both condemned. Many also continue to teach that eternal salvation by faith alone is only New Testament doctrine. Never mind that the subject and context of Romans chapter 11, *"if by grace, then is it no more of works,"* is Israel under the law not realizing that salvation was not of works but of grace.

A curse on details, details are the vermin that destroy great works."

Voltaire (1694-1778)
French Enlightenment writer

The great tragedy of Science: the slaying of a beautiful hypothesis by an ugly fact."

Thomas Henry Huxley (1825 – 29 June 1895)
English biologist and famed evolutionist

This is the great eternal paradox that baffles the self-righteous. The vilest of sinners can be saved while the most observant of the law can be lost. Self-righteousness is the first casualty of the election of grace.

Titus 3:5 **Not by works of righteousness which we have done,** but **according to his mercy** he saved us, by the washing of regeneration, and renewing of the Holy Ghost;

The conclusion to this is obvious: any teaching that works is involved in obtaining or maintaining our salvation nullifies faith and grace. If the gaining of salvation is by God's grace and not by our works, the maintaining of it is also by grace and not works. To be given a free gift and then be told you have to pay to keep it disannuls any semblance of free.

It is the same with grace and works, works to maintain salvation nullifies the free gift of grace.

Romans 4:14 For if they which are of the law be heirs, **faith is made void, and the promise made of none effect:**

Romans 4:16 Therefore **it is of faith, that it might be by grace;**

Any doctrine that teaches that one can earn grace is in error.

Romans 4:4 Now to him that worketh **is the reward not reckoned of grace, but of debt.**

Galatians 5:4 Christ is become of no effect unto you, whosoever of you are justified by the law; **ye are fallen from grace.**

This single precept, *"not by works of righteousness that we have done,"* if adhered to would dissipate many false teachings.

This forms our first precept of the doctrine of salvation.

Salvation is by the grace of God
not by the works of man
neither in the gaining or maintaining thereof

Our precept is not only a principle of New Testament salvation but a general universal precept of God's word. This means that salvation is by grace and not in part or in whole of works at any time, Old Testament, New Testament, Tribulation. Remember that the subject of Romans 11, *"if by grace, then is it no more of works,"*, is Old Testament Israel's failure to understand this precept, God's election of grace.

Even if you had lived a perfect life, from the heart as well as physically, you would only have done what God created you for—your duty.

> *Luke 17:10* So likewise ye, when ye shall have done all those things which are commanded you, say, **We are unprofitable servants: we have done that which was our duty to do**.

> *Ecclesiastes 12:13* Let us hear **the conclusion of the whole matter**: Fear God, and keep his commandments: for **this is the whole duty of man**.

This brings us to the next precept one has to understand to comprehend the doctrine of salvation. Having established that salvation is by grace and in no part based on works, while at the same time realizing that works are our duty to God, not subject to payment or reward or incurrence of debt, we can determine that God is not obligated in any fashion to man.

> *Exodus 33:19* And he said, I will make all my goodness pass before thee, and I will proclaim the name of the LORD before thee; and **will be gracious to whom I will be gracious, and will show mercy on whom I will show mercy**.

> *Romans 9:18* Therefore **hath he mercy on whom he will have mercy, and whom he will he hardeneth**.

Our next precept then must state the position that God is not obligated to save anyone.

Christ's atonement was not an obligation
on God's part to save anyone

This precept, as difficult as it is for some to grasp, is also reflected in passages such as John 3:16, where it states God loved and Christ died to save the world while establishing the condition of *"whosoever believeth."* He died to save the world while that atonement was not an automatic salvation for the world or anyone but given to those that met the condition to believe.

This concept of God's sovereignty might seem a trite, rather obvious truth of Scripture to some. However, there is a large segment of the brethren that do not comprehend the issue of the sovereignty of God correctly. Many errors in teaching are based on the belief that since Christ died for sin someone must automatically have been saved. It is hoped from this study you will see that it is not biblically sound. This mistaken notion is the underpinning of Reformed Theology, Calvinism, or the doctrine of individual predestination as well as Universal Theology, universal salvation. Both theologies are formed by obligating God upon Christ's atonement to automatically save someone. Many faithful saints over the centuries have been confounded by this mistake in reasoning. The truth is, God is not obligated by Christ's atonement to save anyone, it opens the door of salvation to all.

Our last precept in this discussion extends from this point and deals with whom did the Lord give himself for? Although he is not obligated to save anyone he certainly died for someone.

> *2 Peter 3:9* The Lord is not slack concerning his promise, as some men count slackness; but is longsuffering to us-ward, **not willing that any should perish, but that all should come to repentance**.

> *1 John 2:2* And he is the propitiation for our sins: and **not for ours only, but also for the sins of the whole world**.

> *John 12:47* And if any man hear my words, and believe not, I judge him not: for I came not to judge the world, but **to save the world**.

> *Acts 17:30* And the times of this ignorance God winked at; but **now commandeth all men every where to repent**:

> *Ezekiel 18:32* For **I have no pleasure in the death of him that dieth**, saith the Lord GOD: wherefore **turn yourselves, and live ye**.

With these verses we can easily stand on the principle that the atonement for sins was not limited. It is of course a point of contention to some, as above, who reject our second precept. However, this point will not be further suffered. Christ died for the sins of the entire world, all men. Therefore, our next precept states it as such.

Christ's atoning sacrifice
was for the sins of the whole world

Harmonize & Reconcile

**My soul fainteth for thy salvation:
but I hope in thy word.**

—PSALMS 119:81

At this point in the study, we have developed three biblical precepts which are enough to present us with a framework that must be maintained in any description of salvation's methodology.

**Salvation is by the grace of God
and not by the works of man
neither in the gaining**

**Christ's atonement was not
an obligation on God's part
to save anyone**

**Christ's atoning sacrifice
was for the sins of the whole world**

From these precepts, we can compile a list of prerequisites that any interpretation of the doctrine of salvation must incorporate and meet.

- Must be by grace to the exclusion of works

- Must affirm the total inclusiveness of Christ's atonement while allowing for individual exclusion

- Must preserve God's sovereignty in the selection while sustaining universal opportunity of salvation

When we examine this list, we begin to see some of the supposed contradictions that men have stumbled at in forming their theologies. These contradictions become the issues that must be dealt with in our study of salvation's scheme. Two of the main questions that must be contended with are the following:

- How is it that Christ could have died to pay for all sin yet not all be saved?

- How is it that all are eligible and have an equal opportunity to be saved if God in his sovereignty chooses whom he will?

It is these two questions that take us back to the foundation of salvation's plan to attempt to reconcile them.

At first glance, considering much of what is being preached, this would seem to be an insurmountable task, but not so. The following is a portrayal of a design for God's scheme that satisfies these requirements. There can only be one correct biblical interpretation of any doctrine of God's word: *"God is not the author of confusion."* With any doctrine, the interpretation must conform to the requirements of any and all

Scriptures that have any bearing on it. Having now established the requirements that must be incorporated into the scheme of salvation; every verse of Scripture must fit our theology for it to be correct. If a passage of Scripture does not fit, we have something wrong; no forced interpretation of God's word is correct. Our description, therefore, of this doctrine must be simple and unforced in its interpretation; it must easily fall into place meeting all the requirements of the Bible.

Reconciling the apparent contradictions is quite simple. Salvation is analogous to a simple business transaction, the same type of commerce that takes place hundreds of times during a business day among men. Do not be deceived by the transaction's simplicity, regardless of how great the amount being dealt with the exchange is not complex. This description does not trivialize God's salvation. Whether you purchase a twenty-thousand-dollar house or a five hundred million dollar high-rise complex, the transaction is the same. However great the mercy, grace, and price of our salvation the transaction, the exchange, was simple.

> *2 Corinthians 11:3* But I fear, lest by any means, as the serpent beguiled Eve through his subtilty, so **your minds should be corrupted from the simplicity that is in Christ**.

Mankind, as a whole and each of us individually, owed a sin debt to the law of God. Once Adam was corrupted, all that came from him bore that corruption, and we have been doing a fair job of it on our own as well.

> *Job 14:4* Who can bring a clean thing out of an unclean? **not one**.

Christ purchased the total debt of the world. It was no different than when you borrow from a bank. The bank sells the debt, it does not keep your debt. It is the new owners of your debt that you now owe. The bank wanted payment and was paid; the new owners can do with the debt as they please. They can demand payment, or they can forgive it according to their own will and whatever criteria they set. The bank—or in our case, the law—has no more say in the matter.

The law demanded payment for all sin, Christ made that payment. Ownership of our debt was exchanged. The transaction did not include instant or automatic forgiveness of that debt, only a transference of ownership. You can distinguish the transfer by whatever names you care to use, from the law to grace, etc. God's law being satisfied, God can now have mercy on whom he will according to whatever criteria he so desires, his holiness, righteousness, and sovereignty remaining intact and uncompromised.

To confirm the accuracy of the division of payment and forgiveness is simple enough. Throughout the Old Testament, God forgave sin; Christ forgave sin during his earthly ministry. Regardless of that forgiveness, no one was saved, born again, or obtained eternal life thereby. Eternal salvation was not accessible under the old covenant; the sin debt was still owed to the law.

John 7:39 (But this spake he of the Spirit, which they that believe on him **should receive: for the Holy Ghost was not yet given; because that Jesus was not yet glorified**.)

Hebrews 11:13 **These all died in faith, not having received the promises**, but having seen them afar off, and were persuaded of them, and embraced them, and confessed that they were strangers and pilgrims on the earth.

Hebrews 11:39 And these all, having obtained a good report through faith, **received not the promise**:

Without the atonement for sins, there was no salvation regardless of sins forgiven. Further, after the atonement for sins having been made men still died lost. Under the old covenant, those dying having forgiveness for sins were held in escrow, Abraham's bosom. It could not be absent from the body present with the Lord. They were held until the law received payment for sin; the ownership of the debt was transferred. At present, when we receive forgiveness it is immediately effectual: *"absent from the body, ... present with the Lord,"* the payment having been made.

The atonement for sins, great as it was, can best be understood by realizing that it initiated an accounting entry. The sin debt of the world was marked paid in the law column and entered as being owed in the mercy or grace column (or whatever column headings you care to use). The point is it was transferred from absolute damnation to a position of eligibility for salvation where forgiveness of sins was made possible. Men passed from death unto life.

Romans 5:18 Therefore as by the offence of one judgment came upon all men to condemnation; even so by the righteousness of one **the free gift came upon all men unto justification of life**.

Everyone's sin debt to the law was paid making all eligible for forgiveness. Without the atonement, forgiveness would have been ineffectual. Christ died for all and is the means of salvation. Whether or not one finds grace in God's eyes, the forgiveness of their individual sin debt is determined by God's dealing with and judging men's hearts. He has elected that it be by whether one will put their faith in him, in his word, in the testimony and preaching of his Son crucified and raised again. God's sovereignty is preserved in the setting of a condition that men must meet—faith.

Romans 9:15 For he saith to Moses, **I will have mercy on whom I will have mercy, and I will have compassion on whom I will have compassion**.

The Old Testament saints were granted forgiveness of sins based on their faith and trust in God, whether brought about through the preaching of the prophets, the law, or the works that God showed. We now have a greater revelation if not a complete one. That revelation is of God's Son who gave himself that men might receive forgiveness of sin. God, *"not willing that any should perish,"* paid the sin debt for all while not obligating himself to save any. He is free under this plan to establish and set his criteria for his forgiveness of individual sins even after his atonement for all sin.

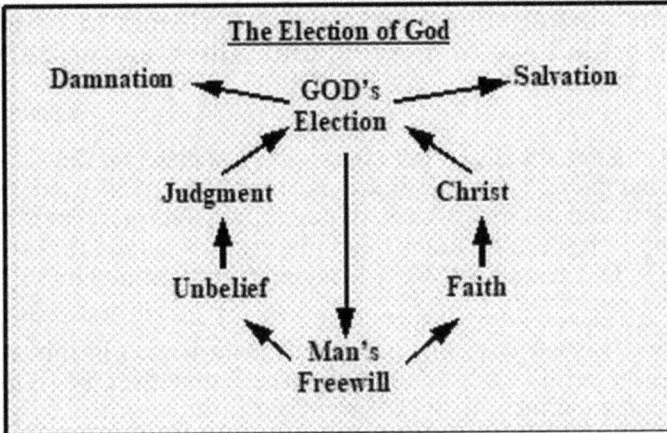

The Election of God

Damnation ← GOD's → Salvation
Election

Judgment   Christ

↑   ↑

Unbelief   Faith

Man's
Freewill

Once one understands the precepts and requirements of the doctrine of salvation it is easy to see how this scheme fits. Its interpretation can be reduced as long as the dual elements of atonement to the law and individual forgiveness are maintained. God paid the price owed to the law satisfying his holiness and righteousness. He now judges the hearts of men to determine whether he will apply that atonement through individual forgiveness maintaining his sovereign will. This scheme of the methodology of salvation satisfies all the requirements of Scripture without any strained or forced interpretations. This methodology of God's salvation must be the foundation that all else is built upon.

We are saved by Christ's atonement upon our meeting the condition of believing in him. Anything other than this dual nature of salvation leads to errors.

Dispensational Salvation

That in the dispensation of the fulness of times he might gather together in one all things in Christ, both which are in heaven, and which are on earth; even in him:

—EPHESIANS 1:10

In this chapter, the differences in salvation at different times in history (or as some prefer) dispensations, is our theme. Salvation by grace through faith and not of works is, of course, a universal precept of God's word being in force at all times in all places. So what are the differences between the Old Testament, New Testament, and Tribulation salvation if any?

The three dispensations or periods of history used in this study are divided as the period from Adam to the crucifixion, the crucifixion to the Rapture, and from there to the return of our Lord.

The discussion of the dispute over the rapture will have to wait until another volume in our series. For now, it will be used as the dividing point between the Church age, or times of the Gentiles, and the Tribulation.

The three modes of salvation that this study will affirm are:

1. **Adam to Cross**—faithful unto death: enduring, keeping faith toward God until the end; reserved unto salvation

2. **Cross to Rapture**—full salvation, liberty in Christ, absent from the body present with the Lord

3. **Tribulation**—faithful unto death: enduring, trusting in God, and not taking the mark until the end to receive salvation

To begin the scriptural underpinnings for these conclusions, what was covered in the preceding chapter must be considered; the Old Testament saints, from Adam to the cross, could not receive full, complete, unconditional salvation because the payment for sin had not been made; Christ had not died for the sins of the world as of yet.

John 7:38-39 He that believeth on me, as the scripture hath said, out of his belly shall flow rivers of living water. [39](But this spake he of the Spirit, which they that believe on him **should receive**: for **the Holy Ghost was not yet given; because that Jesus was not yet glorified.**)

Christ had not died; salvation could not yet be given. The Old Testament saints could have their sins forgiven, but they were not paid for. In fact, as such, they could have their sins laid back upon them if they fell out of grace. In Matthew, a similitude, word picture, is provided of this very situation. The servant's debt was forgiven, but they were laid back on him when he failed to remain in the good graces of his master.

> *Matthew 18:21-35* ²³Therefore is the kingdom of heaven likened unto a certain king, which would take account of his servants. ²⁴And when he had begun to reckon, one was brought unto him, which owed him ten thousand talents. ... ²⁶The servant therefore fell down, and worshipped him, saying, Lord, have patience with me, and I will pay thee all. ²⁷Then the lord of that servant ...**forgave him the debt**. ...³²Then his lord, after that he had called him, said unto him, O thou wicked servant, **I forgave thee all that debt**, ... ³⁴And his lord was wroth, and **delivered him to the tormentors, till he should pay all that was due.**

There was no being sealed with the Holy Spirit; no absent from the body, present with the Lord. They had no liberty in Christ; but those that died in faith were reserved unto salvation and rested in Abraham's bosom until the price for their sins was paid.

> *Luke 16:22* And it came to pass, that the beggar died, and **was carried by the angels into Abraham's bosom**:

The Old Testament saints had to maintain their trust and faith in God unto death where upon they were put in a place of rest awaiting Christ's crucifixion and salvation. Upon that payment, God led captivity captive.

> *Ephesians 4:8* Wherefore he saith, When he ascended up on high, **he led captivity captive**, and gave gifts unto men.

Of course, their sins were forgiven based on faith through grace, faith in whatever God told them at the time. He told Noah there was a flood coming, and Noah, *"moved with fear,"* built the boat. Noah preached to the people; they rejected it. He told Abraham to sacrifice his son, the Israelite's to keep the law, not for self-righteousness but through faith in him who gave it to them.

> *Romans 9:31-32* But Israel, which followed after the law of righteousness, hath not attained to the law of righteousness. ³²Wherefore? **Because they sought it not by faith**, but **as it were by the works** of the law. For **they stumbled at that stumblingstone;**

But what were the promises they could not receive until the payment for sins was completed?

> *2 Corinthians 6:16* And what agreement hath the temple of God with idols? for ye are the temple of the living God; as God hath said, **I will dwell in them, and walk in them**; and I will be their God, and they shall be my people.

> *Ezekiel 36:26-27* A new heart also will I give you, and a new spirit will I put within you: and I will take away the stony heart out of your flesh, and I will give you an heart of flesh. ²⁷And **I will put**

my spirit within you, and cause you to walk in my statutes, and ye shall keep my judgments, and do them.

New Testament salvation is post payment for sins as opposed to pre, Old Testament. New Testament saints upon their faith in the gospel of Jesus Christ receive the promises. They receive and are sealed with the Spirit of God, saved completely and unconditionally forever. It is our liberty in Christ—once saved always saved. Our liberty in Christ is another one of those misunderstood, rarely taught doctrines of the Bible that will have to wait for the next study. Between the cross and the Rapture salvation in full is given to *"whosoever believeth."*

2 Corinthians 1:21-22 Now he which stablisheth us with you in Christ, and hath anointed us, is God; [22]**Who hath also sealed us, and given the earnest of the Spirit in our hearts**.

Ephesians 1:13 In whom ye also trusted, after that ye heard the word of truth, the gospel of your salvation: in whom also after that ye believed, **ye were sealed with that holy Spirit of promise**,

Ephesians 4:30 And grieve not the holy Spirit of God, whereby **ye are sealed unto the day of redemption**.

After the Rapture, the Tribulation period begins. During this time there is no believe on the name of the Lord and thou shalt be saved. At this point it returns to faithful unto death. This means keeping faith in God's word dying a martyr's death for not worshiping or taking the mark of the beast.

Revelation 13:16-17 And **he causeth** all, both small and great, rich and poor, free and bond, **to receive a mark in their right hand, or in their foreheads**: [17]And that no man might buy or sell, save he that had the mark, or the name of the beast, or the number of his name.

Revelation 14:9-11 And the third angel followed them, saying with a loud voice, If any man worship the beast and his image, and receive his mark in his forehead, or in his hand, [10]**The same shall drink of the wine of the wrath of God, which is poured out without mixture into the cup of his indignation**; and **he shall be tormented with fire and brimstone** in the presence of the holy angels, and in the presence of the Lamb: [11]And **the smoke of their torment ascendeth up for ever and ever: and they have no rest day nor night, who worship the beast and his image, and whosoever receiveth the mark of his name**.

During this time, one will have to trust God's word until death; worship the beast, take his mark—you are damned.

Revelation 6:9 And when he had opened the fifth seal, I saw under the altar **the souls of them that were slain for the word of God, and for the testimony which they held**:

Revelation 15:2 And I saw as it were a sea of glass mingled with fire: and **them that had gotten the victory over the beast, and**

over his image, and over his mark, and over the number of his name, stand on the sea of glass, having the harps of God.

The difference between Old Testament and Tribulation salvation is that sins have been paid for, so salvation is granted upon death in faith no need to be kept in reserve.

That is briefly the three dispensations of salvation.

1. **Adam to Cross**—Faithful unto death: trusting in whatever God told you at the time; reserved unto salvation

2. **Cross to Rapture**—Full salvation, liberty in Christ, absent from the body present with the Lord

3. **Tribulation**—Faithful unto death: trusting in God's word not taking the mark; salvation

LIBERTY IN CHRIST

Stand fast therefore in the liberty wherewith Christ hath made us free, and be not entangled again with the yoke of bondage.

—GALATIANS 5:1

Eternal security—can salvation be lost or not? To answer this, ask yourself: what liberty do you have if you can lose your salvation? Somehow the question of our liberty in Christ is never tied to the eternal security of the believer. The answer to the question has eluded many in Christianity since the Dark Ages.

The answer is not difficult to ascertain. The truth in this regard can easily be obtained by referring to the precept established in the study, "Not Of Works." Once it is realized that denying the eternal security of the believer creates a system of salvation based on works, it becomes evident that there is a serious problem with a doctrine whereby one can lose their salvation. It being necessary for those who teach the absence of our security to show a reason for the loss, therefore, it must naturally follow that works apply, if not in gaining, at least in maintaining salvation. However, as the precept, *"Not Of works"* shows, at any time works are added to our salvation, either in the obtaining or maintaining thereof, grace and faith go out the window.

Ephesians 2:8-9 For **by grace are ye saved through faith**; and that **not of yourselves**: it is the gift of God: **Not of works**, lest any man should boast.

A continuing theme throughout the New Testament is the biblical declaration that works and grace are mutually exclusive, one cannot exist with the other. Any teaching that works is involved in obtaining or maintaining our salvation nullifies grace.

Romans 11:6 And **if by grace, then is it no more of works**: otherwise grace is no more grace. But **if it be of works, then is it no more grace**: otherwise work is no more work.

Galatians 3:2-3 This only would I learn of you, Received ye the Spirit by the works of the law, or by the hearing of faith? [3]**Are ye so foolish? having begun in the Spirit, are ye now made perfect by the flesh**?

If the gaining of salvation is by God's grace and not by our works, the maintaining of it must also be by grace and not works. To be given a free gift then being told you have to pay to keep it disannuls any semblance of free. It is the same with grace and works; works to maintain salvation nullifies the free gift of grace as well as faith, God's promises, and Christ's death.

Romans 4:14 For if they which are of the law be heirs, **faith is made void, and the promise made of none effect**:

Galatians 3:18 For **if the inheritance be of the law, it is no more of promise**: but God gave it to Abraham by promise.

Galatians 2:21 I do not frustrate the grace of God: for **if righteousness come by the law, then Christ is dead in vain**.

Any doctrine that teaches that one can earn grace, either in gaining salvation or maintaining it, is in error.

Romans 4:4 Now to him that worketh is the reward **not reckoned of grace, but of debt**.

Galatians 5:4 Christ is become of no effect unto you, whosoever of you are justified by the law; **ye are fallen from grace**.

In this study, a few of the passages of Scripture; Colossians 1:23, Hebrews Chapters 6 and 10 and 2 Peter 2:10-21, which are commonly used to promote the teaching that one can lose salvation will be examined with the knowledge of the biblical precepts established and in keeping with our "Seven Precepts to Understanding the Bible."

The teaching that one can lose salvation is many times restricted to the tribulation saints or the Old Testament Jews to preserve faith without works in this age. Often it is taught, to avoid loss of salvation in this age, that the books Hebrews through Revelation are written to the tribulation Jews only and rightfully only applied to them.

Again, I must point to the mutual exclusiveness of grace and works in any dispensation. The Bible was written to all men. Although, it is comprised of many books, it is one book with one theme and one plan of salvation. There may be parts of Scripture that in application do not belong to the church, such as the old covenant of animal sacrifice or the earthly kingdom given to Israel; except for these types of things everything else applies today to all men everywhere and always has. Sin is still sin, and men have always been in need of a Saviour. Job, being the oldest book in the Bible, testifies to this.

Job 19:25 For **I know that my redeemer liveth**, and that he shall stand at the latter day upon the earth:

Old Testament, New Testament, before Moses, after the Rapture, salvation is still through the shed blood of Jesus Christ and obtained by faith alone.

Unfortunately, you cannot answer most doctrinal questions in a simple verse or two, it takes study and a knowledge of the contents of the whole Bible. When keeping things in context one must preserve the context from the basic sentence, the paragraph, chapter, book, and the whole of the Bible itself. Most, if not all, false teachings are born out of someone's inability or lack of patience in studying and simple misreading of Scripture. Anything less than a sentence in English grammar, or any other language, has no meaning. The sentence is the smallest unit of grammar that possesses definite meaning. A sentence is a trinity; it must have a subject, predicate [verb], and a complete thought. Remember to study it until you comprehend the complete thought.

The following sections are examples of proper Bible study in accordance with the "Seven Precepts to Understanding the Bible."

> Make the word of God as much as possible its own interpreter. You will best understand the word of God by comparing it with itself. *"Comparing spiritual things with spiritual"*
>
> —Sir Isaac Newton 1642-1727
> English Physicist & Mathematician

Colossians 1:23

If ye continue in the faith grounded and settled, and be not moved away from the hope of the gospel, which ye have heard, and which was preached to every creature which is under heaven; whereof I Paul am made a minister;

—*COLOSSIANS 1:23*

This is one of the many occasions where grammar is neglected, for Colossians 1:23 is not a sentence but only part of one. It must be remembered that the sentence is the minimal unit of grammar that maintains definite meaning. The sentence that this phrase is taken out of runs from verse 21 to verse 29, containing 221 words. Admittedly, this sentence can instill a feeling of apprehension in the student of the Bible as when in grade school just the word "grammar" did. Nevertheless, to remove verse 23 from the context of its sentence is to devoid it of any applicable meaning.

The sentence reads as follows:

Colossians 1:21-29 And you, that were sometime alienated and enemies in your mind by wicked works, yet now hath he reconciled, [22]In the body of his flesh through death, to present you holy and unblameable and unreproveable in his sight: [23]If ye continue in the faith grounded and settled, and be not moved away from the hope of the gospel, which ye have heard, and which was preached to every creature which is under heaven; whereof I Paul am made a minister; [24]Who now rejoice in my sufferings for you, and fill up that which is behind of the afflictions of Christ in my flesh for his body's sake, which is the church: [25]Whereof I am made a minister, according to the dispensation of God which is given to me for you, to fulfill the word of God; [26]Even the mystery which hath been hid from ages and from generations, but now is made manifest to his saints: [27]To whom God would make known what is the riches of the glory of this mystery among the Gentiles; which is Christ in you, the hope of glory: [28]Whom we preach, warning every man, and teaching every man in all wisdom; that we may present every man perfect in Christ Jesus: [29]Whereunto I also labour, striving according to his working, which worketh in me mightily.

This sentence is enough to make a school child tremble. However, it is quite simple if the context of the whole chapter is maintained.

Colossians 1:10 **That ye might walk worthy of the Lord** unto all pleasing, being fruitful in every good work, and increasing in the knowledge of God;

93

This is one of the many sentences in Scripture that try our heart's desire to study; it certainly must be rightly divided. This sentence simplified, without modifiers and side tracking, and in normal order, reads as follows:

He (Christ) hath now reconciled you to present you holy and unblameable and unreproveable in his sight.

As for the phrase in question:

If ye continue in the faith grounded and settled, and be not moved away from the hope of the gospel,

The subject matter in Colossians has nothing to do with losing salvation, but as being saved, continuing in righteousness so that our Lord may present you holy, unblameable and unreproveable in his sight. Compare this with Ephesians.

Ephesians 5:25-27 Husbands love your wives, even as Christ also loved the church, and gave himself for it; [26]That he might sanctify and cleanse it with the washing of water by the word, [27]**That he might present it to himself a glorious church, not having spot, or wrinkle, or any such thing; but that it should be holy and without blemish**.

In Colossians 1:21, it states that the Lord reconciled us to himself, this reconciliation was our salvation.

Romans 5:10 For if, when we were enemies, we were reconciled to God by the death of his Son, much more, **being reconciled**, we shall be saved by his life.

2 Corinthians 5:18-19 And all things are of God, **who hath reconcile** us to himself by Jesus Christ, and hath given to us the ministry **of reconciliation**; [19]To wit, that God was in Christ, **reconciling** the world unto himself, not imputing their trespasses unto them; and hath committed unto us **the word of reconciliation**.

Colossians 1:20 And, having made peace through the blood of his cross, by him **to reconcile** all things unto himself; by him, I say, whether they be things in earth, or things in heaven.

In verse 22 of our text, it states that his purpose is, *"to present you holy and unblameable and unreproveable in his sight."* or as Ephesians puts it, *"That he might present it to himself a glorious church, not having spot, or wrinkle, or any such thing; but that it should be holy and without blemish."* Now being cleansed by the blood of Christ, it is up to each individual to remain *"unblameable and unreproveable in his sight."*

2 Peter 3:14 Wherefore, beloved, seeing that ye look for such things, **be diligent that ye may be found of him in peace, without spot, and blameless**.

This is what preaching and teaching to the saints is for, to keep them from spotting themselves; it is the washing of our feet.

> *John 13:10* Jesus saith to him, **He that is washed needeth not save to wash his feet**, but is clean every whit: and ye are clean, but not all.

> *Colossians 1:28* Whom **we preach, warning** every man, and **teaching** every man in all wisdom; **that we may present every man perfect in Christ Jesus**:

Works have nothing to do with salvation, everything to do with whether a saint remains holy, unspotted, and blameless.

> *Corinthians 5:10* For **we must all appear before the judgment seat of Christ**; that every one may receive the things done in his body, **according to that he hath done, whether it be good or bad**.

Colossians 1:23 has nothing to do with losing salvation.

Hebrews Chapters 6 & 10

For it is impossible for those who were once enlightened, and have tasted of the heavenly gift, and were made partakers of the Holy Ghost, And have tasted the good word of God, and the powers of the world to come, ⁶If they shall fall away, to renew them again unto repentance; seeing they crucify to themselves the Son of God afresh, and put him to an open shame. For the earth which drinketh in the rain that cometh oft upon it, and bringeth forth herbs meet for them by whom it is dressed, receiveth blessing from God:

—*Hebrews 6:4-7*

For if we sin wilfully after that we have received the knowledge of the truth, there remaineth no more sacrifice for sins, ²⁷But a certain fearful looking for of judgment and fiery indignation, which shall devour the adversaries.

—*Hebrews 10:26-27*

The explanation of these verses is again not difficult, it simply requires keeping everything in context. These verses cannot be taken without some small amount of thought. All one has to do is take notice that there is no explanation within any one of the verses to explain who they are talking about. Therefore, they must be put back in context. The old questions once taught in school (whether they still do I know not) still apply: who, what, where, when, why, and how. Before you can understand a verse of Scripture you must have the answers to all these questions.

> I had six honest serving men,
> They taught me all I knew,
> Their names were Where and What and When
> And Why and How and Who.

—*Kipling, Rudyard (1865-1936) English journalist, writer*

The secret, for lack of a better word, to understanding the book of Hebrews, to rightly dividing the book, is comprehending that there are no major divisions in it. There is no change of topic or subject. The entire book, except for the closing, is concerned with the same subject from the first chapter to the last. Although written from a Jewish viewpoint, the book is for everyone; it is the book of Romans chapters 1-7 from a Jewish perspective. It is a comparison between the old and new covenants. It begins with telling how God spoke under the old, in the past, and how he now speaks through his Son. It goes on to explain who the Son is and how he is worthy of more glory than Moses or angels. It compares the old priesthood with the new priesthood of Christ, the blood of bulls and goats with the blood of Christ; it shows that the way was not shown, under the first covenant, into the holy of holies. It compares the imperfection of the law and its requirements to that of the body, Jesus Christ, that God hath prepared for an acceptable sacrifice. Hebrews also demonstrates that the Old Testament saints were saved by faith just as the New (chapter 11).

However, the great comparison in the book of Hebrews is the comparison between belief and unbelief, faith in God and not having faith in God. If you will keep the verses in question in the context of their chapters, and the entire book, it is easy to see that this comparison is the subject of the passages questioned here.

Take chapter 10 and look at the last verse:

Hebrews 10:39 But we are not of them **who draw back unto perdition; but of them that believe to the saving of the soul**.

It tells you plainly that it is not the saved who are being spoken about, but those *"looking for a fearful judgment,"* in verses 20 and 21, no one has lost it. The *"drawing back unto perdition"* is not believing unto salvation. Who are those then being spoken of? They are compared to those that *"despised Moses' law."*

Hebrews 10:28-29 He **that despised Moses' law** died without mercy under two or three witnesses: [29]Of how much sorer punishment, suppose ye, shall he be thought worthy, **who hath trodden under foot the Son of God**, and **hath counted the blood of the covenant, wherewith he was sanctified, an unholy thing, and hath done despite unto the Spirit of grace**?

The comparison is between believers and non-believers, *"we are not of them who draw back unto perdition; but of them that believe to the saving of the soul."* They are they who are equated with those who *"despised Moses' law"* and who have treated God's Holy Spirit of grace contemptuously and have trodden underfoot the Son of God.

Examine and determine the context of the entire book of Hebrews:

Hebrews 3:12 Take heed, brethren, lest there be in any of you an **evil heart of unbelief**, in departing from the living God.

Hebrews 3:19 So we see that they could **not enter in because of unbelief**.

Hebrews 4:6 Seeing therefore it remaineth that some must enter therein, and they to whom it was first preached entered **not in because of unbelief**:

Hebrews 4:11 Let us labour therefore to enter into that rest, lest any man fall after the **same example of unbelief**.

The whole book of Hebrews is an exhortation to believe the gospel.

Hebrews 4:2 For unto us was the gospel preached, as well as unto them: but the word preached did not profit them, **not being mixed with faith in them that heard it**.

Yes, the gospel was preached and rejected by those spoken about being condemned in 10:26-27. Chapter 6 is no different, it is a continuation of the belief-unbelief comparison.

Hebrews 6:9 But, beloved, we are persuaded better things of you, and **things that accompany salvation**, though we thus speak.

The better things are things that *"accompany"* or are brought about by salvation. All Israel was enlightened and tasted the heavenly gift and were partakers of the Holy Ghost, but many did not believe and fell away from the truth. The world and especially this nation have tasted also.

Hebrews 6:18-19 That by two immutable things, in which it was impossible for God to lie, we might have a strong consolation, who have fled for refuge to lay hold upon **the hope set before us**: [19]Which hope we have **as an anchor of the soul, both sure and stedfast**, and **which entereth into** that within the veil;

There should be no need to say more. If you will read the book of Hebrews through from start to finish a few times without stopping and get the context settled, it is self-evident. Too many people read the Bible one verse at a time and never put anything into context.

2 Peter 2:20-21

For if after they have escaped the pollutions of the world through the knowledge of the Lord and Saviour Jesus Christ, they are again entangled therein, and overcome, the latter end is worse with them than the beginning. For it had been better for them not to have known the way of righteousness, than, after they have known it, to turn from the holy commandment delivered unto them.

—2 PETER 2:20-21

2 Peter 2:20-21 will close out this study of eternal security. This passage is one of the staples of the lose your salvation teaching.

It will be found that the same thing is true here in this chapter as in our other passages, the verses are taken out of context. The subject of the chapter is as there were false prophets, there are false teachers. Again, it is a comparison, a double comparison; the false teachers of chapter 2 contrasted against the holy men of the preceding chapter being comparable with the false prophets of the Old Testament.

> *2 Peter 2:1* But there were false prophets also among the people, **even as there shall be false teachers among you**, who privily shall bring in damnable heresies, even denying the Lord that bought them, and bring upon themselves swift destruction.

Verse nine gives us the comparison again.

> *2 Peter 2:9* The Lord knoweth how to deliver **the godly** out of temptations, and to reserve **the unjust** unto the day of judgment to be punished:

Verses 10, 12, and 17 tell us who is being spoken about.

> *2 Peter 2:10* But chiefly **them that walk after the flesh in the lust of uncleanness, and despise government. Presumptuous** are they, **selfwilled**, they are **not afraid to speak evil of dignities**.

> *2 Peter 2:12* But these, as natural brute beasts, made to be taken and destroyed, **speak evil of the things that they understand not**; and shall utterly perish in their own corruption;

> *2 Peter 2:17* These are **wells without water, clouds that are carried with a tempest**; to whom the mist of darkness is reserved for ever.

This is not the description of a saved man; these never understood. It is the false teachers; it is their judgment being spoken of.

> *2 Peter 2:3* And **through covetousness shall they with feigned words make merchandise of you**: whose judgment now of a long time lingereth not, and their damnation slumbereth not.

Read chapter 1, you will see that chapter 2 is just a continuation and the comparison is between those holy men God spoke to, who accepted God's word, and these false teachers that do not. To further cinch this contention that no one is losing their salvation the Lord gives us the example of Lot for us to understand the security of the believer.

2 Peter 2:7-8 And delivered just Lot, vexed with the filthy conversation of the wicked: [8](For **that righteous man** dwelling among them, in seeing and hearing, vexed **his righteous soul** from day to day with their unlawful deeds;

What is Lot's testimony of faith toward God? He certainly is not one of the heroes of the faith of Hebrews chapter 11. He was greedy and materialistic. His family so unaccustomed to righteous living and teaching about God that the one time he is shown to preach the truth, his children think he is drunk or out of his mind. He had chosen to live and remain among the sodomites for his gain, to the detriment and loss of his own family. One time and one time only is Lot shown to have had faith in what God said: when he was told to flee the wrath to come. He did not live godly before, nor is there any record of him doing so after, yet he is described as a *"righteous"* man. He is put here to emphasize that God is not condemning the saved. No one is losing salvation in this chapter nor anywhere else in the Scriptures.

Romans 8:1 **There is** therefore now **no condemnation to them which are in Christ Jesus**, who walk not after the flesh, but after the Spirit.

Romans 8:9 But ye are not in the flesh, but in the Spirit, **if so be that the Spirit of God dwell in you.** Now **if any man have not the Spirit of Christ, he is none of his**.

When the Spirit of God made his abode in the sinner, the sinner passed from death unto life; there is no going back.

John 5:24 Verily, verily, I say unto you, He that heareth my word, and believeth on him that sent me, **hath everlasting life, and shall not come into condemnation; but is passed from death unto life**.

1 John 5:12 He that hath the Son **hath life**; and he that hath not the Son of God **hath not life**.

If the Scriptures were to be taken out of context, it would be a forced conclusion that the only way to lose your salvation would be to try and keep it by works.

Galatians 5:4 Christ is become of no effect unto you, whosoever of you are justified by the law; **ye are fallen from grace**.

One can make the Bible teach anything by taking its passages out of their context—

context, Context, CONTEXT

CALVINISM
ARMINIANISM
NEO-ARMINIANISM
OPEN THEOLOGY
FOREKNOWLEDGE OF GOD

INTRODUCTION

Remember the former things of old: for I am God, and there is none else; I am God, and there is none like me, Declaring the end from the beginning, and from ancient times the things that are not yet done, saying, My counsel shall stand, and I will do all my pleasure: Calling a ravenous bird from the east, the man that executeth my counsel from a far country: yea, I have spoken it, I will also bring it to pass; I have purposed it, I will also do it.

—ISAIAH 46:9-11

The frame of mind brought to the study of the Bible is dependent on two main theological questions whose answers determine the main bias held or the framework through which its understanding is confined and filtered through. To approach the Bible with a more meaningful understanding and be fully outfitted as a soldier in the battle for the truth of the Scriptures it is essential to understand and answer these questions correctly.

The questions concern individual salvation and God's foreknowledge: what does he know, when did he know it, and how does he know it? At this point, the thought that God is omniscient, knows everything, is blinding some to the truth and it is this that created the differing theologies that divide Christianity. God certainly knows all there is to know; the debates and divisions are over that which is not there to be known. How does he know what has not happened as yet, or does he? What if God does not want to know all from start to finish but wants some things to play out like a man's thoughts and desires? Can God give things a life of their own where he has to wait to see what that life will do? Would it be limiting God to say he can or cannot do something according to his own choice?

Psalms 78:41 Yea, they turned back and tempted God, and **limited the Holy One of Israel**.

It is not a question of what God can or cannot do; he can do whatever he wants, however he wants; it is for man to seek that which he has revealed within the Scriptures to find out what that is.

Amos 3:7 Surely the **Lord GOD will do nothing, but he revealeth his secret unto his servants the prophets**.

It is all in God's word. Nevertheless, without an open mind, the Bible remains sealed, a book of confusion and contradiction.

Two questions:

Is individual salvation predestinated or do men have free will?

Is history closed— completed, fixed, unchanging, or is it open running in real time?

These are the two questions that divide Christianity. Over the next few pages, an attempt will be made to explain such in a meaningful simple understandable manner.

Points To Ponder

But strong meat belongeth to them that are of full age, even those who by reason of use have their senses exercised to discern both good and evil.
—*HEBREWS 5:14*

How the questions under consideration are answered determines whether the Bible is open and understood correctly. Again, those questions are:

> Is individual salvation predestinated or do men have free will?

> Is history closed—completed, fixed, unchanging, or is it open running in real time?

These two questions divide Christianity into four main theologies which must be discernable and understood to rightly divide the word of truth. These are foundational theologies and although there are many mix-and-match teachings, once these four are understood the rest will be easy to figure out. The four are:

- Reformed (Calvinism, Sovereign Grace, Presbyterianism)
- Arminianism
- Neo-Arminianism
- Open Theology

Reformed	Arminian	Neo-Arminian	Open Theology
Predestination	Predestination	God Sees All	In Real Time
Limited Atonement	Open to All	Open to All	Open to All
Total Depravity	Total Depravity	Free Will	Free Will
History Closed	History Closed	History Closed	History Open

The bare essence of these theologies is all that is of interest; only the essential parts needed to compare them to each other and equate them to the Scriptures.

Many are familiar with these theologies, however, Neo-Arminianism, new-Arminianism, may be unfamiliar. It is a designation made here to identify what many refer to as being Arminian to confirm they are not Calvinistic in the doctrine of predestination, not realizing Arminianism was not against Calvinism's predestination but only a slight modification to it. A name was needed to distinguish those that were truly against predestination and neo-Arminianism seemed appropriate.

Arminianism modified Calvinism by incorporating a test prior to election. Each individual was given prevenient faith, a little faith preceding election to see which way an individual leaned: toward or away from God. This test was given to all hence salvation open to all in opposition to Calvinism's limited atonement. If you leaned toward God, you were elected and predestinated to be saved. Predestination and total depravity still prevailed.

Predestination theologies strongly premise their view on the supposition that if all is not predetermined by God then he would not be sovereign. It would be hard to find a more unreasoned, unbiblical, assertion. God is the Creator and sustainer of all things; how can he not be sovereign in whatever he does or chooses to do? Regardless of what he elects to do, it would be his sovereign will. He would be just as sovereign, if after creation, he sat back in an easy chair to watch what happened. To insist on anything else would be to limit God.

> *Psalms 78:41* Yea, they turned back and tempted God, and **limited the Holy One of Israel**.

This is a major error in the premise of predestination; God does not like to be described as limited.

Even those advocating predestination admit that their doctrine contradicts many passages of Scripture. Any time a teaching conflicts with the obvious meaning of a passage of Scripture it is a clear sign that some part of it is in error. The Bible does not contradict itself. The clear and obvious meaning of the following verses dismisses the doctrine of Calvinism's limited atonement.

> *John 3:14-17* And as Moses lifted up the serpent in the wilderness, even so must the Son of man be lifted up: [15]That **whosoever believeth in him** should not perish, but have eternal life. [16]For God so loved **the world**, that he gave his only begotten Son, that **whosoever believeth in him** should not perish, but have everlasting life. [17]For God sent not his Son into **the world** to condemn **the world**; but that **the world** through him might be saved.

Romans 10:13 For **whosoever** shall call upon the name of the Lord shall be saved.

1 John 2:2 And he is the propitiation for our sins: and **not for ours only, but also for the sins of the whole world**.

➢ *Propitiation*, if you are unfamiliar with it means atonement.

Acts 17:30 And the times of this ignorance God winked at; but now commandeth **all men every where** to repent:

1 Timothy 4:10 For therefore we both labour and suffer reproach, because we trust in the living God, **who is the Saviour of all men, specially of those that believe**.

These verses are clear and obvious in their meaning. The atonement was made for all men everywhere, all humanity, not limited, and those that believe get the benefit. Nonetheless, with these and many other such examples, the Reformed doctrine admits the contradictions with their teaching but continues holding to limited atonement.

There are attempts to reconcile predestination and free will to achieve both. One such effort is to promote the idea that men have free will, but God's sovereign will trumps it. If God does not approve of a free will choice, he will rewire the person so he will make the free will choice of God's choosing. They think this preserves God's sovereignty and man's free will. It seems to fall short. One example given is as follows:

> The 41st President of the United States of America, George H. W. Bush, reportedly hates brocolli so intensly that he simply refuses to eat it under any circumstances. There is no chance of him choosing it, not because he is a robot or a puppet, but because he hates it. If you had the power to change his tastes such that he suddenly loved brocolli, you could effectively predetermine whether or not he would ever eat it:
>
> a. If you chose to leave him as he is, and not change his tastes, you would be effectively dooming him to brocolliless (sic) meals forever! You could count on the fact that he would always shun it of his own free will.
>
> b. If you elected to step in and change his tastes, you would be effectively assuring that he would eat it. If he began to love it, he would seek it out of his own free will.
>
> George's free will remains intact, and you make certain your will is done, with no contradiction. [6] (I believe he means both God's sovereign will and George's free will remain intact.)

---

6. David J. Finnamore; elevenmistrel.com;
http://www.elvenminstrel.com/kontext/misunderstandingsofsovereigngrace.htm

It is not sure if the author of that illustration understands what a contradiction is. It is not free will if God dictates what that free will is.

The lack of understanding of the extent and limits of free will has been a debilitating factor in understanding the issues of many of the teachings of Scripture. The idea that man has free will to do as he pleases is utterly unbiblical. Man has free will of desire, inclination, passion, aspirations, motivation, intention: likes, dislikes, loves, hatreds. He does not have free will of action, only of the thoughts and intents of his heart.

> *Hebrews 4:12* For **the word of God** is quick, and powerful, and sharper than any twoedged sword, piercing even to the dividing asunder of soul and spirit, and of the joints and marrow, and **is a discerner of the thoughts and intents of the heart**.

All actions must serve God's purpose and be within the confines of the master plan.

> *Matthew 10:29* Are not two sparrows sold for a farthing? and **one of them shall not fall on the ground without your Father**.

> *1 Samuel 2:3* Talk no more so exceeding proudly; let not arrogancy come out of your mouth: for the LORD is a God of knowledge, and **by him actions are weighed**.

The creator and sustainer of all is in control of all actions taken upon the earth. It may be that a desire is allowed to be acted upon, the Lord may use the actions desired by the thoughts and intents of the heart for his purposes, or acting upon a thought or intent may not be allowed.

> *James 4:13-15* Go to now, ye that say, To day or to morrow we will go into such a city, and continue there a year, and buy and sell, and get gain: [14]**Whereas ye know not what shall be on the morrow**. For what is your life? It is even a vapour, that appeareth for a little time, and then vanisheth away. [15]**For that ye ought to say, If the Lord will, we shall live, and do this, or that**.

It would not be difficult for the Lord to find someone with the right thoughts and intents of the heart to serve his purpose in any given circumstance.

> *Romans 9:17* For the scripture saith unto Pharaoh, Even **for this same purpose have I raised thee up**, that I might shew my power in thee, and that my name might be declared throughout all the earth.

Do you think it was hard to find a haughty-minded, lifted-up-with-pride, selfish, self-centered, self-willed, individual who regarded neither man nor God to set upon the throne? It would have been harder to find one that was not.

> *1 Timothy 4:15* **Meditate upon these things**; give thyself wholly to them; that thy profiting may appear to all.

A man's free will desires are developed not by one mental or physical attribute (e.g., his taste buds) although they are a consideration. Free will is developed by the events, education, training, and experiences, in a man's life. What you would choose of your own free will at five is not going to be the same at twenty, and that may not be the same at forty, fifty, sixty, etc. For God to change your free will choices is to predetermine your choice removing your free will.

This is the only proper biblical understanding of free will and must be adhered to in order to maintain *"rightly dividing the word of truth."*

To understand and evaluate these theologies it is essential to examine the differences in their view of history. Of the two questions: is individual salvation predestinated or do men have free will, and is history closed (i.e., completed, fixed, unchanging) or is it open running in real time, the answer to the second will solve the dilemma. These different concepts of history lead to the questions about God's foreknowledge: what God knows, how he knows it, and when he knows it?

In the case of Calvinism and Arminianism, all is predetermined, unchangeable, history is closed, from before the foundation of the world. God's foreknowledge is due to his having predestinated all things. This would hardly be meaningful to mankind. There is nothing men can do but follow a predetermined path; they are born, get elected or not, then they die. There were a few, some famous, gospel preachers of the Reformed religion but they were Reformed in name only; they acted and preached as if it made a difference, as non-predestinationist.

An analogy might be a road map. Predestination's map, Reformed and Arminianism, would have but one road, one route, going from one predetermined place and event in a row to the next: point A to B to C to D to E, etc. All things are predestined, history is static, fixed, unchanging, everything is set in stone. The choices men make are not real, the options given them meaningless; everything is predetermined. That pretty much sums up what is needed to know of the doctrine of predestination. Many attempts are made to try reconciling predestination with the Bible; it would be preferred if your teaching was in accordance with and did not have to be reconciled to the Scriptures.

Moving on, it is now time to look at the free will theologies.

Still setting forth the idea that history is closed, complete, unchanging, Neo-Arminianism rejects predestination. God's foreknowledge comes from his looking at the past, present, and future all at once thereby seeing history and all that happened. Individual salvation not being predestinated but just known to God who will and will not be saved as he sees history as it just happened to happen.

Neo-Arminianism's map has many ways to go to reach the same predetermined points and events. The course taken is neither divinely determined nor guided; when the trip is over, God sees all and goes back and inserts himself and writes a book about the travels he has taken particular interest in. There are some latent problems in this view. Two considerations must be addressed and explained. If not predestinated, for God not to have knowledge of all history, it would have to exist apart from God, flowing out on its own undetermined course; how did it come into existence? History would have had to have run its course for God to see what happened. Further, would God inserting himself into the past change the future? Would it cause men to have different free will choices changing what God had already seen? How many changes need to take place before the future God saw was no longer valid?

This led one commentator, in reference to 1 Samuel 23: 10-13, to claim that the unchangeable foreknowledge of God can be changed.

> David broke the unchangeable foreknowledge of God by escaping the city before Saul came and everything God said about that future was changed.[7]

It would seem that neo-Arminianism's view of history creates some unanswerable questions and, as predestination, puts limits upon God.

Open Theology has history running in real time under the control and guidance of God, directing all to his predetermined end; there would be no limits to what he could choose to do.

Open Theology's road map has the same trip to make, the same fixed predetermined events to happen, same set waypoints to reach, and it ends at the same preestablished conclusion to all things. However, it is fluid; man's decisions and actions make a difference in how history is played out in between the predetermined events and waypoints. There is more than one road to take in reaching them. There are at least two ways of getting there; obey God and take the easy direct route, or disobey him and take the circuitous undulating treacherous route due to God's judgment upon your disobedience. Both closed and open theology lead to the same place; it is just how you get there. Open leaves room for time and chance and God's judgments upon and dealings with men in real time to determine and set their course on the fly.

> *Ecclesiastes 9:11* I returned, and saw under the sun, that the race is not to the swift, nor the battle to the strong, neither yet bread to the wise, nor yet riches to men of understanding, nor yet favour to men of skill; but **time and chance happeneth to them all**.

The idea that God must look down upon history to see what happen is the most lackluster God limiting view of these theologies. In Open Theology having history flow in real time, raises the Lord to heights the others cannot even imagine. Working in real time, knowing every thought

---

[7] "The Book of Romans", Dr. Peter S. Ruckman, 2003ISBN 1-58026-045-4, Romans 8:29-30, pg. 333.

and intent of men as they have them in the moment, knowing all things as they happen, having them in control, guided, and kept within his plan, God turns everything, all Satan's devises, his and man's evil intents, to his purpose. He judges and passes judgment on all and records all in his books, all in real time. It is mind-boggling; man cannot fathom the depths of the wisdom and power of the Almighty.

> *Romans 11:33* O **the depth of the riches both of the wisdom and knowledge of God**! how unsearchable are his judgments, and his ways past finding out!

> *Daniel 4:35* And all the inhabitants of the earth are reputed as nothing: and he doeth according to his will in the army of heaven, and among the inhabitants of the earth: and **none can stay his hand, or say unto him, What doest thou**?

As for David's being able to change the unchangeable foreknowledge of God, Open Theology asserts that it is no more a matter than God's searching men's hearts and knowing their thoughts thereby knowing what they would do in any given situation. David did not change the unchangeable foreknowledge of God; he changed the situation by leaving after being warned of God of what would happen according to the *"thoughts and intents of the heart"* of the men involved if he stayed.

> *1 Chronicles 28:9* for the LORD **searcheth all hearts, and understandeth all the imaginations of the thoughts**: if thou seek him, he will be found of thee; but if thou forsake him, he will cast thee off for ever.

God's plan or blueprint is laid out with its predetermined waypoints and events. He will guide and direct all things as needed to keep all within his plan. In Open Theology there is room for time and chance, spontaneity, more importantly for God's dealing with men and nations, raising them up and tearing them down through judging and judgment upon them. There are always at least two ways to reach the waypoints: fear God and obey or rebel and pay.

God discerners the thoughts and intents, weighs all possible actions and outcomes, and determines the course he is going to take in real time, in accordance with his criteria, keeping all within his master plan and outline. Speaking of rain, Job writes:

> *Job 37:13* He causeth it to come, whether **for correction**, or **for his land**, or **for mercy**.

If the wrong view or bias is accepted, it will cloud and color the correct interpretation of all Scripture while the right one will open the Bible. Viewing the Bible from a perspective of predestination will read that into verses everywhere and incorporate it into all understanding and interpretations removing all personal responsibility. On the other hand, teaching that all history is just there and unchanging would lead to the acceptance of fate eliminating personal responsibility. Open Theology leaves room for God to act in the moment, to hold men responsible, to test men, to judge men, and for time and chance.

WHAT SAYETH THE SCRIPTURE

**These were more noble than those in
Thessalonica, in that they received the word
with all readiness of mind, and searched the
scriptures daily, whether those things were so.**

—ACTS 17:11

Many concepts and teachings are based on philosophy rather than the
diligent study of God's word. Philosophy is the attempt to reason a
knowledge of God and his ways without studying his revelations, precepts, or teachings in their proper context. Just read a verse and determine an interpretation that seems to fit distilled through your bias, your
biblical view, without comparing scripture with scripture. However,
God's ways and thoughts are past the ability of man to fathom without
his revelations and instructions.

> *Romans 11:33* O the depth of the riches both of the wisdom and
> knowledge of God! **how unsearchable are his judgments, and
> his ways past finding out!**

To privately interpret a verse is to interpret it apart from its context
and apply whatever meaning fits based on the bias you bring. To properly
understand a portion of Scripture, context must be maintained, not only
that of the passage but the chapter, book, and the entire Bible. If any
portion of Scripture fails to fit within or contradicts our theology or
teaching, there is something wrong with it. A modification needs to be
made or an outright rejection of it; the Bible should not be rejected or
changed to make it fit.

In some instances, it is a mistake to rely on biblical understandings,
interpretations, and traditions that were formed hundreds, or even thou-
sands, of years ago without the benefit of the knowledge currently known
of creation, prophecy, and history. All things are revealed within the
Scriptures, but not all made known from the beginning nor have they
been revealed at the same time throughout history.

> *Luke 24:45* Then **opened he their understanding**, that they might
> understand the scriptures,

> *Daniel 12:4* But thou, O Daniel, shut up the words, and **seal the
> book, even to the time of the end**: many shall run to and fro, and
> **knowledge shall be increased**.

In 1909 Charles Peguy thought that "the world changed less since
Jesus Christ than in the last thirty years", and perhaps some young

doctor of philosophy in physics would now add that his science has changed more since 1909 than in all recorded time before.[8]

Civilization has made its greatest strides in the last thousand years, and in the last three centuries, man's rate of development seems almost to have increased by geometric progression.[9]

What would these historians say today? Can it be said that those interpreting the Bible in the past had the same knowledge available now in their attempts to correctly do so?

> *Ephesians 3:4-5* Whereby, when ye read, ye may understand my knowledge in the mystery of Christ) [5]**Which in other ages was not made known unto the sons of men, as it is now revealed** unto his holy apostles and prophets by the Spirit;

I would think that it must be asked; was everything totally revealed and understood in the past? Has not knowledge increased? Is not more known about creation than those that came before?

It does not matter how longstanding something is, many errors are longstanding. Who or how many hold to an understanding does not prove it. God has always parceled out the light of his word and knowledge in general at his scheduled rate and purpose. Many times raising a man up to be the focal point (e.g., Moses, monotheism; Paul the Church; Martin Luther and others breaking from Catholicism; Peter S. Ruckman preservation of the AV 1611). This does not mean that they were the first or only people to hold those views, right in all their views, or necessarily any godlier than anyone else.

In the next few sections, several competing theologies are going to be examined in the light of Scripture and reason.

---

[8] Will & Ariel Durant. The Lessons of History, chapt. 1, pg. 12, , Simon & Schuster, NY, 1968, ISBN 0-671-41333-3

[9] Vern L. Bullough, Man in Western Civilization, Holt Rinehart & Winston, inc., (1957) 1970; SBN:: 03-077015-7

The Potter

The word which came to Jeremiah from the LORD, saying, Arise, and go down to the potter's house, and there I will cause thee to hear my words.

—JEREMIAH 18:1-10

Several passages of Scripture are used to attempt to justify predestination; Romans 9:18-21, the similitude of the Potter is invariably used.

> *Romans 9:18-21* Therefore **hath he mercy on whom he will have mercy**, and **whom he will he hardeneth**. [19]Thou wilt say then unto me, **Why doth he yet find fault**? For **who hath resisted his will**? [20]Nay but, O man, who art thou that repliest against God? Shall the thing formed say to him that formed it, Why hast thou made me thus? [21]**Hath not the potter power over the clay, of the same lump to make one vessel unto honour, and another unto dishonour?**

In this passage, the potter is a similitude comparing God as the creator of man to the potter as the creator of his vessels. As the potter can choose to make one vessel honorable and another dishonorable so God can create a man thus. The question is whether this similitude is supposed to be teaching predestinated individual salvation? The precepts and general truths, established in the preceding chapters, ought to tell us that such an interpretation is automatically wrong. For the moment, these precepts and truths will be disregarded in simply comparing scripture with scripture, rightly dividing. Let us see what the conclusion of the matter will be.

That it is God's word and not man's must be remembered. He uses the similitude of the potter first in the Old Testament, so seeking its proper interpretation must begin in its original context and entirety to properly decipher its true biblical meaning in the new. Remember, God is not the author of confusion, the intent of both uses will be the same.

> Jeremiah 18:1-10 The word which came to Jeremiah from the LORD, saying, [2]Arise, and go down to **the potter's house**, and there I will cause thee to hear my words. [3]Then I went down to the potter's house, and, behold, he wrought a work on the wheels. [4]And the vessel that he made of clay was marred in the hand of the potter: so he made it again another vessel, as seemed good to the potter to make it. [5]Then the word of the LORD came to me, saying, [6]O house of Israel, **cannot I do with you as this potter**? saith the LORD. Behold, as the clay is in the potter's hand, so are ye in mine hand, O house of Israel. [7]At what instant I shall speak concerning a nation, and concerning a kingdom, to pluck up, and to pull down, and to destroy it; [8]**If that nation, against whom I have pronounced, turn from their evil, I will repent of the evil that I thought to do unto them**. [9]And at what instant I shall speak

concerning a nation, and concerning a kingdom, to build and to plant it; [10]**If it do evil in my sight, that it obey not my voice, then I will repent of the good, wherewith I said I would benefit them**.

In the similitude of a potter presented in the above passage, it can be easily seen that it is not an attempt to teach predestination in any form but rather just the opposite. God's decisions are based on the choices made by man, whether to seek and obey God or to do evil. Paul did not, and neither can we, take a passage of Scripture out of its context but must rightly divide the word of truth. The context, in Jeremiah as in Romans, is the sovereignty of God over his creation, to judge and deal with it according to his will.

If we take the passage in Romans and keep it within its proper context, we see that the similitude is given in answer to three particular questions.

- Is there unrighteousness with God?
- Why does he yet find fault?
- Who can resist his will?

Looking closely, we find that these questions are being asked by those who are complaining about God not accepting their self-righteousness—that is in keeping the law they have not obtained or earned the grace of God and the assurance of salvation. By their way of thinking, if salvation is solely based on the predetermination and/or caprice of God and not on a person's works, how can he find fault? For who can resist his will? How is he just in this? Paul's answer is simply to point out that God is our Creator, and he could just as easily have created us for damnation as not, therefore, there is no unrighteousness in God's judgments, which is the question in verse 14 of Romans 9.

Romans 9:14 What shall we say then? **Is there unrighteousness with God**? God forbid.

If we refuse to accept his salvation it is the same to God as if he had created us unto damnation; your predestinated end in such a case is the same, eternal wrath.

The similitude of the potter is not a description of God's plan of salvation, but rather an example of our relationship to him and his sovereignty. He made us and he can do as he pleases with us; there is no unrighteousness in whatever he does. It is for us to fear him and seek that which is pleasing unto God. It is not a picture of God's plan, but of his prerogative as the creator to choose his own plan of salvation, one that pleases him and our duty to conform. The actual plan God has elected to institute is not mentioned until the last verse of the chapter, *"whosoever believeth."*

Romans 9:33 As it is written, Behold, I lay in Sion a stumblingstone and rock of offence: and **whosoever believeth on him** shall not be ashamed.

This also answers the proverbial question that lost sinners ask in their attempt to make themselves more just than God: you mean that God would condemn a heathen in the jungle who has never heard of Jesus Christ? The answer is if God chooses to do so, there is no unrighteousness with God; it is his prerogative, he made us, he can do whatever he wants with us. What we, as those who have trusted in God's word, have to worry about is the other side of the coin: God is going to hold us responsible for that heathen not hearing about Jesus Christ, whether he lives in a jungle or is our neighbor. We ought to be thankful that he is *"not willing that any should perish,"*

Conforming

There is therefore now no condemnation to them which are in Christ Jesus, who walk not after the flesh, but after the Spirit.

—*ROMANS 8:1*

One mistake often encountered when Romans 8 is under consideration is its being referenced and applied to the state of an individual Christian's walk, whether a brother or sister is walking after the flesh or the Spirit, serving or not serving God. However, the subject of the chapter has absolutely no bearing as to whether an individual Christian is living right or not. The chapter is a summary of the seven chapters that came before it, *"There is therefore."* The chapter is a summary of what salvation is and is not, as explained in the previous chapters. It compares men as a group in their natural state walking after the flesh with saved men as a group walking after the Spirit. When it talks about being in the Spirit, it is speaking of being saved: when it speaks of being after the flesh, it is speaking of being lost.

Romans 8:9 But **ye are not in the flesh, but in the Spirit**, if so be that **the Spirit of God dwell in you**. Now if any man have not the Spirit of Christ, he is none of his.

The common mistake of applying it to a saint's personal life already clouds the understanding of the context of this chapter by putting individuals in where there are none. A Christian's behavior and manner of living does not come into play until Romans 12. At that point, because of all that has come before (chapters 1-11) Paul states he implores each individual saint to serve God. Until Romans 12:1, the book has been a description and definition of what salvation is, is not, does, and does not include. Up till this point, Romans deals with men as sets—the set of believers as opposed to the set of non-believers—and that does not change in verses 8:29-30, which are the subject of this section.

Up till this point Romans deals with men as sets—the set of believers as opposed to the set of non-believers—and that does not change in verses 8:29-30 which are the subject of this section.

Romans 8:5 For **they** that are **after the flesh** do mind the things of the flesh; but **they that are after the Spirit** the things of the Spirit.

Romans 8:14 For **as many as are led by the Spirit of God**, they are the sons of God.

There is nothing that points to God speaking of each and every individual that ever was or any individual, whether predestined or just known. As stated, chapter 8 is a summary of the first seven chapters.

Paul goes on to talk about the glory of salvation and the waiting for its glorious completion.

Romans 8:18-28 For I reckon that the sufferings of this present time are not worthy to be compared with **the glory which shall be revealed in us**. [19]For the earnest expectation of the creature waiteth for the **manifestation of the sons** of God ... [21]Because the creature itself also shall be **delivered from the bondage of corruption** into the glorious liberty of the **children** of God ... [23]And not only they, but ourselves also, which have the firstfruits of the Spirit, even **we** ourselves groan within ourselves, waiting for **the adoption**, to wit, **the redemption of our body** ... [28]And **we** know that all things work together for good to **them** that love God, to **them** who are the called according to his purpose.

Why do all the above come into play? Because God predestinated us? No. The passage might not be referring to men conforming to anything.

All these things come into play because God predestinated himself, the Word, to be manifested in the flesh, conformed to the image of his Son, and pay for our sins. Romans 8:29 is a description of salvation, of the Word becoming flesh and our part in that predestination as a group. It might just be God, the Word, that had to be conformed to the right image.

Romans 8:29 For **whom he did foreknow**, he also did predestinate to be conformed to the image of his Son, that he might be **the firstborn among many brethren**.

John 1:14 And **the Word was made flesh**, and dwelt among us, (and we beheld his glory, the glory as of the only begotten of the Father,) full of grace and truth.

Hebrews 10:5 Wherefore when he cometh into the world, he saith, Sacrifice and offering thou wouldest not, but **a body hast thou prepared me**:

Philippians 2:7 But made himself of no reputation, and took upon him the form of a servant, and was made in the likeness of men:

Hebrews 2:9 But we see Jesus, who was **made a little lower than the angels** for the suffering of death, crowned with glory and honour; that he by the grace of God should taste death for every man.

The biblical definition of a son of God is one who was directly created or begotten by God in his image, which leaves out everything but Adam, angels, and Jesus Christ.

Luke 3:38 Which was the son of Enos, which was the son of Seth, which was the son of Adam, which was **the son of God**.

Job 38:7 When the morning stars sang together, and all **the sons of God** shouted for joy?

Adam and the angels were directly created by God individually with the ability to reproduce, pro-creation. The angels were not given the liberty to do so, nor were they given what Adam was given so he could— *Eve*. This did, as you remember, cause some problems a little later.

> *Matthew 22:30* For in the resurrection they neither marry, nor are given in marriage, but are as the angels of God in heaven.

> *Genesis 6:2* That the sons of God saw the daughters of men that they were fair; and **they took them wives** of all which they chose.

What is the image of the sons of God, the angels? They are indistinguishable from men.

> *Hebrews 13:2* Be not forgetful to entertain strangers: for thereby some have **entertained angels unawares**.

Man was created in the image of God; Adam was a son of God. We never lost the image; we did lose the relationship.

> *Genesis 5:3* And Adam lived an hundred and thirty years, and begat a son **in his** own **likeness, after his image**; and called his name Seth:

God created Adam to be in his image; Adam reproduced children in his own image, which bore his image of God.

> *James 3:9* Therewith bless we God, even the Father; and therewith curse we men, which **are** **made after the similitude of God**.

"Men, which are made after the similitude of God," but either not being directly created by God were not sons of God, or God chose not to extend the relationship due to the fall. This does not change the assertions that sin had a corrupting effect on the physical form such as in the matter of blood, etc. Adam had a Spiritual birth, but not a water birth. His children had a water birth, but not a Spiritual one. Our salvation is the receiving of the spiritual birth and to be adopted and become sons of God. We do not have to be conformed to become the sons of God; we just need to be adopted.

> *John 1:12* But as many as received him, to them gave he power to **become the sons of God**, even to them that believe on his name:

This does not require conformity to another image. We do not need to be conformed to an image; we need to *"present our bodies a living sacrifice."* Any conforming we need will take place in the resurrection, when *"we shall be changed."* Our spiritual bodies will bear the image of man and God as the angels.

> *Luke 24:39* Behold my hands and my feet, that it is I myself: handle me, and see; for **a spirit hath not flesh and bones**, as ye **see me have**.

"For whom he did foreknow"—we know that he foreknew the Word; we know that the Word had to conform to an image *"a little lower than*

an angels," *"made in the likeness of men"* to suffer death for us all. This is indisputable. Our predestination is part of the Word's predestination. The Word as the Son of God was predestinated to have many brethren. Romans 8:29 is a complete sentence which is a trinity: subject, verb, and complete thought. Verse 30 is a sentence with its own complete thought: it picks up at the end of verse 29. The Word was predestinated to be conformed to the image of a man and to be the firstborn from the dead and to have many brethren. Verse 30 picks up with the many brethren of verse 29 and completes their predestination to certain things. The two verses make a complete reference and description of salvation in accordance with the context of the entire book of Romans up to this point.

> *Romans 8:29-30* For whom (**The Word**) he did foreknow, he also did predestinate to be conformed to the image of his Son, that (**the Word**) might be the firstborn among many brethren. [30]Moreover (**the many brethren**) whom he did predestinate, them he also called: and whom he called, them he also justified: and whom he justified, them he also glorified.

Four other verses use the words predestinated or foreknowledge and they all refer to the plan of salvation, not individuals. Why would we expect Romans 8:29-30 to be any different?

> *Acts 2:23* Him, being delivered by **the determinate counsel and foreknowledge of God**, ye have taken, and by wicked hands have crucified and slain:

> *Ephesians 1:5* Having **predestinated us unto the adoption of children** by Jesus Christ to himself, according to the good pleasure of his will,

> *Ephesians 1:11* In whom also **we have obtained an inheritance, being predestinated according to the purpose** of him who worketh all things after the counsel of his own will:

> *1 Peter 1:2* Elect **according to the foreknowledge of God** the Father, **through sanctification of the Spirit, unto obedience and sprinkling of the blood of Jesus Christ**: Grace unto you, and peace, be multiplied.

All these are speaking of different aspects of the predestinated plan of salvation. Christ was predestinated to make the atonement; men were predestined to be saved through the sanctification of the Spirit and blood of Jesus Christ. Those that receive salvation are predestined to be adopted and receive an inheritance as children of God. Romans 8:29-30 is also a description of the plan of Salvation.

Rightly Dividing

The words of the LORD are pure words: as silver tried in a furnace of earth, purified seven times.
Psalms 12:6

"God is not the author of confusion." In Romans 8:29 it could have been stated; "For those, he did foreknow," if it was referring to the "them" of verse 30. He could have stated; "Conformed to the image of the Son," and sealed the interpretation. The words God chose to use in writing his revelation were purposely selected, purified seven times, there is nothing random in his choice of them. Possibly, we should not look for an interpretation that God could have made perfectly obvious in stating it a little differently and look for one that would only exist because he stated it the way he did.

> *Romans 8:29* For whom he did foreknow, he also did predestinate to be conformed to the image of **his** Son, that he might be the firstborn among many brethren.

If you study the New Testament's use of the terms, *"his Son"* compared to *"the Son,"* you will see that whenever the term *"his Son"* is used, it is always indirect reference to God or action of God in relation to Christ Jesus. Whenever the term *"the Son"* is used, it is in reference to everything other than God, e.g., men, Satan, demons, etc. to Christ Jesus.

> *John 3:16-17* For **God** so loved the world, that he gave **his** only begotten Son, that whosoever believeth in him should not perish, but have everlasting life. [17]For **God** sent not **his Son** into the world to condemn the world; but that the world through him might be saved.

God gave, God sent ... **his** Son

> *Matthew 4:3* And when **the tempter** came to him, **he said**, If thou be **the Son** of God, command that these stones be made bread.

Satan uses ... **the** Son

> *Acts 3:13* The **God** of Abraham, and of Isaac, and of Jacob, the God of our fathers, hath **glorified his Son** Jesus;

God glorified ... **his** Son

> *Romans 1:4* And **declared** to be **the Son** of God with power, according to the spirit of holiness, **by the resurrection** from the dead:

Declared by the resurrection ... **the** Son

> *1 Corinthians 1:9* **God** is faithful, by whom ye were **called** unto the fellowship of **his Son** Jesus Christ our Lord.

God called ... **his** son

> *2 Corinthians 1:19* For **the Son** of God, Jesus Christ, who was preached among you by us, even by me and Silvanus and Timotheus, was not yea and nay, but in him was yea.

Paul and others preached ... **the** Son

> *Galatians 4:4* But when the fulness of the time was come, **God** sent forth **his Son**, made of a woman, made under the law,

God sent ... **his** Son

> *Galatians 2:20* I am crucified with Christ: nevertheless **I** live; yet not **I**, but Christ liveth in me: and the life which I now live in the flesh **I** live by the faith of **the Son** of God, who loved me, and gave himself for me.

I (Paul) ... **the** Son

> *Galatians 4:6* And because ye are sons, **God hath sent** forth the Spirit of **his Son** into your hearts, crying, Abba, Father.

God sent ... **his** Son

> *Ephesians 4:13* Till **we all** come in the unity of the faith, and of the knowledge of **the Son** of God, unto a perfect man, unto the measure of the stature of the fulness of Christ:

We all ... **the** Son

> *1 Thessalonians 1:10* And to wait for **his Son** from heaven, whom **he raised from the dead**, even Jesus, which delivered us from the wrath to come.

God raised ... **his** Son

> *1 John 5:10* **He** that believeth on **the Son** of God hath the witness in himself: he that believeth not God hath made him a liar; because he believeth not the record that **God** gave of **his Son**.

He (whoever) believeth on ... **the Son**; **God gave** record of ... **his Son**

Any of those verses could be rewritten to use the other term. The separation of the terms is purposeful, not an accident, not random. Romans 8:29 in using the term *"his Son"* tells us that God is performing some action related to *"his Son,"* and neither man nor anything else is involved. It is not man that has to be conformed; if it were the term used would have been *"the Son."*

> *Romans 8:29* For whom he (**God**) did foreknow, **he** (**God**) also did predestinate to be conformed to the image of **his** Son, that he might be the firstborn among many brethren.

Accordingly, when the Bible speaks of God in relation to Christ Jesus, the term used is *"his Son."* When speaking of man or any other in relation to Christ Jesus, the term used is *"the Son."* Man is not being spoken of in Romans 8:29; man is not being predestinated, not the one conforming; God as the Word is. God sent, God raised, God spoke through, God predestinated *"his Son."*

Attention to detail, keeping in context, not having an unbiblical view and corrupted bias is what is needed in studying the Scriptures.

CLOSING REMARKS

Wherefore seeing we also are compassed about with so great a cloud of witnesses, let us lay aside every weight, and the sin which doth so easily beset us, and let us run with patience the race that is set before us,

—*HEBREWS 12:1*

In the last few pages, the two questions that divide the Church have been examined.

1. Predestination verses Free Will

2. Closed verses Open

I have not covered all the debates and arguments for or against any of the four possible theologies that stem from the debates. They have been displayed in their basic forms to show their strengths and weaknesses. My conclusions, if not having been made known at this point, to answering the questions are these.

1. Free Will

2. Open

I do not believe the Scriptures support any other determination.

Open Theology's assertions, that history is flowing in real time, that the future has not yet been, and that God is directing historic events to his predetermined end while along the way dealing with and judging men in real time, conforms to all Scripture. God is dealing with the hearts of men as they come into existence through God's created system of pro-creation. All men came into this world by *"time and chance."*

Ecclesiastes 9:11 but **time and chance happeneth to them all**.

The foreknowledge presented by Open Theology is of God's elections, how he has chosen to do things. That they can be spoken of as future, present, or past according to God's perspective at the time he is speaking is due to the fact that the events are written in stone, immutable. They will come to pass on time as planned, nothing in heaven or earth can prevent them. This is what Satan has been attempting to do from the beginning of his rebellion—*break God's word*.

An analogy can be made to a supercomputer playing chess. At all times it knows the constraints and boundaries of play and every move the pieces can make and every change created by any possible move that happens. The computer may figure things out to three, four, or more moves ahead. It also knows every response it can make per each possible move made and the changes to possible moves they make.

God knows everything there is to know at any given time and every possibility, every possible move by six billion plus men, creature, and nature, etc. He knows all the possible moves and all his possible responses, etc. How far ahead he takes it, who knows! He knows the hearts and minds of men and their propensities, frailties, weaknesses, strengths, etc. He is also dealing with men's hearts seeking to save.

God allows men a limited amount of free will in the moves they make. If God is not at the time purposely directing an event, man's free will choice can make a time and chance event for someone else. As an example, I decide on my own free will to quit or retire from a job; this would make a time and chance job opening for someone else. On the other hand, God could just as easily be directing me to leave a job and create a job for someone in answer to prayer.

God's direction, man's free will, and time and chance, all work together under God's guidance and control. He is not having any difficulty controlling events to suit his purposes in having mercy or judgment upon the earth and leading all things to his predetermined end. God does not have to see what has been done to know what men will do, he knows their hearts and minds. History must be open and flowing for God to deal with and attempt to change the mind and hearts of men. The God of Open Theology is much greater than those of Calvinism, Arminianism, or neo-Arminianism.

Predestination's gospel of limited atonement and its irresistible grace is a different gospel from that of neo-Arminianism and Open Theology's open to all conditioned on our free will choice to believe God. Anyone being saved in a Calvinistic setting is being so despite that doctrine and due to the preaching of the gospel: *"believe on the Lord Jesus Christ and thou shalt be saved."*

Calvinism, even with its teaching of limited salvation, has had some great soul-winning preachers who associated themselves with the reformed doctrine but still maintained the necessity to preach the gospel to all men (e.g., C. H. Spurgeon, Reformed Baptist). As one of the old Reformed preachers is reported to have stated, the more he preached the gospel, the more people were elected. God's sovereign will remains uncontested in the absence of individual predestination. He has chosen, elected, as his sovereign will, to save those that will believe. He will have mercy on them to salvation and those that will not believe, he will not.

One of the simplest and most poignant answers to the question of limited atonement was in an old sermon by Frederick Whitfield, first preached circa 1850s, *"The Apostolic Call and Commission."*

> *"And they came unto Him."* Here is the evidence of our calling and election. We come because He calls. Let us not trouble ourselves with the doctrine of election. Let each one ask himself the question; Have I come to Jesus? If you have, reader, then Christ has called you, and

you have heard that call. You are one of the elect, for you have come to Jesus. To ask the question; Am I one of the elect? first ask another; Have I come to Jesus? But if there are two questions in the matter of salvation, such is the perversity of the human heart, that men are certain to ask the wrong one first. Am I one of the elect? is not the first question, reader. Have I come? ask that first. Your answer to this question will be the answer—the only answer—to the other. Oh, have you come to Jesus? Have you heard His call? Are you at His feet?[10]

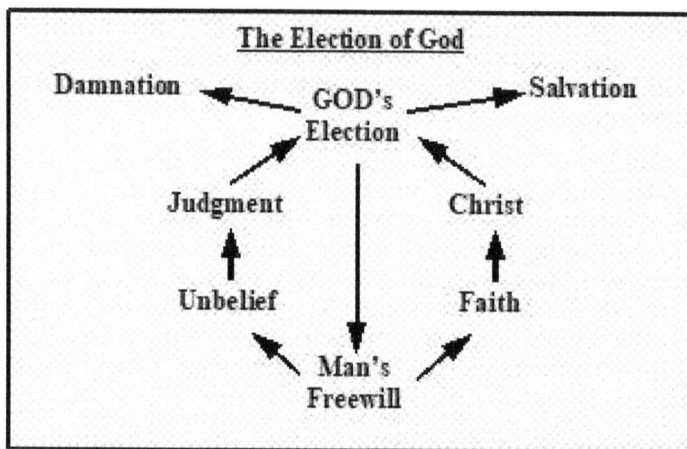

The Election of God

Whether one chooses neo-Arminianism or Open Theology, as long as grace through faith is maintained, it will not change the effect on salvation, does not alter any major doctrine. The results are the same even if one must adjust his thinking on how something was done. It is the indirect that must be considered. The wrong option might be a little leaven that is trying to leaven the whole lump; which in these present days could be troublesome. Open Theology is the only one that does not limit God or create contradictions.

Psalms 78:41 Yea, they turned back and tempted God, and **limited the Holy One of Israel**.

It is for each one of us to take the time to diligently study God's word and determine for ourselves what option corresponds best with Scripture. Let us not be as those who learn something the wrong way and stick to it no matter what, refusing to yield to the truth.

One error many people make is to learn something the wrong way and stick to it no matter what.

Harry Lorayne, Secrets of Mind Power (1961)

---

[10]https://aficj.org/index.php/articles/bible-studies/11-life-service/12-apostolic-call-and-commission

Much more could be said on the questions discussed in this study. It is hoped that enough information has been imparted to give a basic understanding of them and the importance of having the correct framework from which to study the Bible. For whatever context, with whatever bias, you approach God's word will color the deeper study and understanding of it.

Let me present a summary of what I hope to have demonstrated up to this point.

1. Biblical Christianity is unique among the world's religions.

2. That there is a true church and a false church.

3. That there are biblical precepts that must be understood and followed to understand the Bible.

4. Like a puzzle, the Bible pieces must be put together a little here and a little there, line upon line, precept upon precept in building our understanding and doctrines.

5. That salvation by grace through faith is a two-part process; Christ Jesus died for all, but each has to come independently. This removes any supposed contradiction in God's plan of salvation.

6. That salvation is by God's grace through our faith at any time in history.

7. That you need the right biblical view: free will, by Grace through Faith, history is Open.

8. At this time in history, the times of the Gentiles or church age, we have liberty in Christ from the fear of condemnation—once saved, always saved.

In the following chapters, I am going to take what I have asserted up to this point and study out two more recent teachings that in my opinion are in error to such an extent that they can only be described as perverting the gospel. I hope, even if you are a practitioner of them, that all will give the following a fair, open-minded, scriptural consideration. Lay aside any bias and let the Scriptures speak for themselves.

THEOLOGY
OF
GRACE

INTRODUCTION

**But we believe that through the grace of the Lord
Jesus Christ we shall be saved, even as they.**

—ACTS 15:11

A significant portion of the Christian brotherhood regards salvation by grace through faith as not only a New Testament doctrine but a doctrine that was first instituted with the calling out of Paul and his ministry to the Gentiles. Grace Theology, the subject of this study, sometimes referred to as hyper-dispensationalism, contends that there are two gospels, one for Gentiles and a different one for Jews. Within the purview of Grace Theology, there is a variety of teachings, variations on the same theme, some even as far as stating that Paul was the first person saved by grace without works and/or the first person to be put into the body of Christ, the Church. Trying to correlate the variety of different variations can be quite difficult.

Due to that difficulty, the focus of this study will be concerned with the basic assertions or cornerstones of this theology. The main tenet of Grace Theology is that Paul preached a different gospel to the Gentiles than Christ Jesus, Peter, John, James, and others to the Jews.

It is not certain whether all adherents of Grace Theology preach two gospels today. If it is taught that there is still a Jewish gospel different from Paul's that must be preached to Israel today, then it would indeed be deceitful and pernicious. If they believe in two different gospels today then the gravity of the error reaches the definition of heresy. It is difficult to filter as not all teachings concerned with Grace Theology by its different advocates agree with each other. This theology is certainly not being singled out on this point as it is the same with most theologies; this can make it difficult to discuss the common ground within any of them. The differences within Grace Theology are of no consequence to this study as it will be shown that there never were two gospels of salvation.

Grace Theology is defined here as believing that salvation by grace through faith without works was a mystery given to Paul for the times of the Gentiles and that our Lord, Peter, John, James, Matthew, Luke, and the Jewish believers preached to the Jews a different gospel. This difference is such that some teach that John chapter 3 (John 3:16) is a Jewish gospel that will not lead to gentile salvation today.

In this study, several aspects of the teaching of Grace Theology will be compared to the Scriptures.

1. **The Gospels**—are there more than one?

2. **Works**—can they save?

3. **Dispensations**—is grace but one of many?

4. **Mysteries**—is the gospel one?

Men tend to learn something the wrong way and stick to it no matter what for many reasons, all bad, rather than learn to diligently study, rightly divide God's word, and prove all things for themselves. There is no growing in knowledge and understanding without constant reexamination and making needed changes to what you thought you knew.

The contention over this teaching, as all the battles over God's word, is spiritual. The same assertions of defending the word, rightly dividing, and holding to the King James Version will be made on all sides. It is important to keep in mind the confusion and division within the Church two gospels have had and remember that God is not the author of confusion.

1 Corinthians 14:33 For **God is not the author of confusion**, but of peace, as in all churches of the saints.

Hebrews 12:2 Looking unto Jesus **the author and finisher of our faith**; who for the joy that was set before him endured the cross, despising the shame, and is set down at the right hand of the throne of God.

The Gospel

For I am not ashamed of the gospel of Christ: for it is the power of God unto salvation to every one that believeth; to the Jew first, and also to the Greek.
Romans 1:16

There are several gospels mentioned within the Scriptures:

Matthew 4:23 **the gospel of the kingdom,**

Mark 1:1 **the gospel of Jesus Christ**, the Son of God;

Romans 10:15 **the gospel of peace,**

Mark 1:14 **the gospel of the kingdom of God,**

Acts 20:24 **the gospel of the grace of God.**

Romans 1:1**the gospel of God,**

Romans 10:15 **the gospel of peace,**

Galatians 2:7 **the gospel of the uncircumcision ... the gospel of the circumcision**

Ephesians 1:13 **the gospel of your salvation:**

Revelation 14:6 **the everlasting gospel**

The best definition for the word 'gospel' is—truth. It is the truth concerning the topic at hand.

Ephesians 1:13 In whom ye also trusted, after that ye heard **the word of truth**, the gospel of your salvation:

To understand the Scriptures, any differences between one gospel from another, if there are any, should be determined.

Only one gospel concerns us at this point, *"the gospel of your salvation."* It must be determined whether Christ Jesus, Peter, James, John, and all the others preached the same gospel of salvation as Paul, Barnabas, Mark, Silas, and the other Jews and Gentiles that ministered with Paul: that salvation is by grace through faith and not of works.

Are there two different gospels of salvation? This is our first question to be resolved.

Jesus was the *"Lamb slain from the foundation of the world."*

Revelation 13:8 And all that dwell upon the earth shall worship him, whose names are not written in the book of life of **the Lamb slain from the foundation of the world.**

There is only one lamb slain from the foundation of the world, one plan of salvation, one sacrifice for sins.

> *Hebrews 10:12* But this man, after he had offered **one sacrifice for sins for ever**, sat down on the right hand of God;

The gospel of Christ being born of a virgin, our sins being laid on him, his dying for them, and being raised from the dead, are all subjects of prophecy throughout the Old Testament taught before he was born. Paul himself states the truth of this fact.

> *1 Corinthians 15:3-4* For I delivered unto you first of all that which I also received, how that Christ died for our sins **according to the scriptures**; [4]And that he was buried, and that he rose again the third day **according to the scriptures**:

Paul's gospel was not a mystery *"kept secret since the world began."* It was according to the Scriptures and at that time it could only be a reference to the Old Testament.

> *Amos 3:7* Surely the **Lord GOD will do nothing, but he revealeth his secret unto his servants the prophets**.

> *John 5:39* **Search the scriptures**; for in them ye think ye have eternal life: and **they are they which testify of me**.

It is necessary to compare the gospel preached by the Lord, Peter, John, et. al. The gospel of salvation that the Lord preached was that you had to believe in him, what he said about himself, and what he was going to do.

> *John 8:24* I said therefore unto you, that ye shall die in your sins: for **if ye believe not that I am he**, ye shall die in your sins.

> *Mark 8:31* And he began to teach them, that the Son of man must suffer many things, and be rejected of the elders, and of the chief priests, and scribes, and **be killed, and after three days rise again**.

> *Mark 8:31* the Son of man must **suffer many things, and be killed, and after three days rise again**.

> *John 3:14-16* And as Moses lifted up the serpent in the wilderness, **even so must the Son of man be lifted up**: ... [16]For God so loved the world, that **he gave his only begotten Son**, that **whosoever believeth in him** should not perish, but have everlasting life.

> *Matthew 27:63* Saying, Sir, we remember that that deceiver said, while he was yet alive, **After three days I will rise again**.

Our Lord preached to believe in him and that he was to be crucified, die, be buried, and rise the third day.

Compare the above preaching of Christ's with that of Paul's:

1 Corinthians 15:1-4 Moreover, brethren, I declare unto you the gospel which I preached unto you, ... how that **Christ died for our sins...** [4]And that **he was buried, and that he rose again the third day according to the scriptures**:

What is the difference? Is there a difference simply due to the Lord pointing to it in the future and preaching believe it and Paul's pointing to it in the past and preaching believe it? Are they two different gospels?

John 8:28 Then said Jesus unto them, When ye have lifted up the Son of man, **then shall ye know that I am he,**

"Then shall ye know." It was to the Jews that Christ stated that they would know the truth after he made his sacrifice. Naturally, if they had been understood and enlightened beforehand they would not have crucified him.

1 Corinthians 2:8 Which none of the princes of this world knew: for **had they known it, they would not have crucified the Lord of glory**.

There may seem to be differences in the administration of the gospel before and after his resurrection which is understandable as no one could receive the Holy Spirit before he made the atonement. The way had to be prepared for the understanding of the gospel.

John 7:39 (But this spake he of the Spirit, which they that believe on him should receive: for **the Holy Ghost was not yet given; because that Jesus was not yet glorified**.)

Hebrews 11:13 These all died in faith, **not having received the promises**,...

Ezekiel 36:27 And I will **put my spirit within you**,...

It is taught by some that John the Baptist's preaching is the same as that of Christ, Peter, John, James, etc. This is not true. John the Baptist was not preaching the gospel of salvation but the remission, personal forgiveness, of sins in preparation for the gospel; he was preparing the way to it.

Matthew 3:3 For this is he that was spoken of by the prophet Esaias, saying, The voice of one crying in the wilderness, **Prepare ye the way of the Lord**, make his paths straight.

John preached baptism for the remission of sins. Remission of sins is not salvation; it is forgiveness of sins. Remission, forgiveness, of sins is only half of what you need for salvation. John the Baptist was preparing the way for the other half. The other half is faith in the atonement for sins, the payment for sins: *"Behold the Lamb of God, which taketh away the sin of the world."*

When the Lord arrived on the scene. he preached that he was the fulfillment of the prophecies concerning the Messiah, that he must suffer,

134

die, and rise from the grave on the third day. The particulars of the gospel he preached are the same as the one Paul preached.

The Jews were waiting for their Messiah and the restoration of their kingdom, *"gospel of the kingdom."* Until the martyrdom of Stephen in Acts and Israel's rejection of Christ as Saviour; the great commission and bringing in the kingdom were the next items on the agenda.

The only difference in the gospels before and after the atonement at this point is that before they were told they would receive the Holy Spirit, and after, we are told we have received the Spirit. Does that make them different gospels? This causes some misunderstandings in the book of Acts. At the stoning of Stephen, Israel as a nation is set aside for later and the individual transition from the old covenant into the new covenant of the Church consisting of Jew and Gentile continues.

In the book of Acts, a couple of transitions take place owing to this division in being able to receive the Holy Spirit. One transition concerns those believing or receiving the remission of sins by John's baptism before the atonement. They now had to be led to and baptized unto the resurrected Lord obtaining the atonement and full salvation from sin. Baptism for the remission and forgiveness of sins could be given before the atonement. Then after one would be pointed to faith in Christ and be baptized unto him to receive the atonement for sin, the Holy Spirit, and full salvation. Sin having been paid for, we are pointed after the atonement to faith in Christ for the remission of our sins receiving the baptism of the Holy Spirit and full salvation. This is done all with one gospel: believe on the Lord Jesus Christ that he will, or has, died for our sins will be or was buried and will or has risen again the third day, depending on if it is before or after the atonement.[11]

Another disputed proof text of Grace Theology is that the gospel of the circumcision is different from the gospel of the uncircumcision as found in Galatians.

> *Galatians 2:7-9* But contrariwise, when they saw that **the gospel of the uncircumcision** was committed unto me, as **the gospel of the circumcision** was unto Peter; [8](For he that wrought effectually in Peter to the apostleship of **the circumcision**, the same was mighty in me toward **the Gentiles**:) [9]And when James, Cephas, and John, who seemed to be pillars, perceived the grace that was given unto me, they gave to me and Barnabas the right hands of fellowship; that we should go unto **the heathen**, and they unto **the circumcision**.

The teaching that the two gospels in Galatians are different is the product of taking the terms out of the context of not only their sentence but chapter, book, and the Bible as a whole.

---

[11] See chapter "Salvation," pg 91.

The correct interpretation of the phrases *"the gospel of the circumcision"* and *"the gospel of the uncircumcision"* is found by keeping the context of chapter 2 and not forgetting what you should have just read in chapter 1.

> *Galatians 1:6-7* I marvel that ye are so soon removed from him that called you into **the grace of Christ** unto **another gospel**: [7]Which is not another; but there be some that trouble you, and would **pervert the gospel of Christ**.

Paul states that it is not another gospel the Galatians are getting messed up with but a perversion of the gospel of the grace of God. They are backsliding; now that they are saved, they think they have to keep the law to keep their salvation.

> *Acts 15:5* But there rose up certain of the sect of the Pharisees which believed, saying, That **it was needful to circumcise them, and to command them to keep the law of Moses**.

> *Galatians 3:2* This only would I learn of you, Received ye the Spirit **by the works of the law**, or **by the hearing of faith**?

It is obvious that Paul is preaching the same faith he persecuted.

> *Galatians 1:23* But they had heard only, That he which **persecuted us** in times past **now preacheth the faith which once he destroyed**.

Take note also that it was not Gentiles but the Jewish Christians he was persecuting.

> *Acts 9:1-2* And Saul, yet breathing out threatenings and slaughter against the disciples of the Lord, **went unto the high priest**, [2]And desired of him letters to Damascus to the synagogues, that if he found any of this way, whether they were men or women, **he might bring them bound unto Jerusalem**.

Roman Gentiles did not come under the control of the Jewish High Priest so the gospel he preached was the same one that he persecuted which was the same gospel the Jews were saved by.

Later in Galatians chapter 2 Paul shows again that there is but one gospel for Jew and Gentile. Peter was visiting and thoroughly enjoying the fellowship of the Gentiles in so much that he was eating with them, described by Paul as living like them. When Peter heard that some Jewish believers sent from James were coming, he decided he needed to be a Jew again.

> *Galatians 2:11-12* But when Peter was come to Antioch, I withstood him to the face, because he was to be blamed. [12]For before that certain came from James, **he did eat with the Gentiles**: but when they were come, he withdrew and **separated himself, fearing them which were of the circumcision**.

Paul takes notice and rebukes the Jews for trying to make two gospels and reminds them there is but one.

> *Galatians 2:14* But when I saw that they walked not uprightly **according to the truth of the gospel,**

In rebuking Peter for trying to divide the gospel into two—one Jewish, one Gentile—Paul gives a dissertation on the Jewish gospel.

> *Galatians 2:15-16* We who are Jews **by nature, and not sinners of the Gentiles,**

We, Paul says, being natural-born Jews and not Gentile converts.

> [16]Knowing that a man **is not justified by the works of the law, but by the faith of Jesus Christ,**

We, Jews, know that no man is justified by the works of the law, but salvation is through grace by faith in the Lord Jesus Christ.

> *Acts 15:11* But **we believe** that through the grace of the Lord Jesus Christ **we shall be saved,** even as they.

> even we have believed in Jesus Christ, that we might be justified by the faith of Christ, and not by the works of the law: for by the works of the law shall no flesh be justified.

As Paul states, we being Jews, know that no works can save us, that there is but one gospel preached by Paul, Peter, James, John, and the Lord Jesus Christ. There are two ministries, one to the Jews and one to the Gentiles. This is by no means absolute as both Paul and Peter preached to both Jew and Gentile.

> *Ephesians 2:11-17* Wherefore remember, that ye being **in time past Gentiles** in the flesh, who are **called Uncircumcision** by that which is called **the Circumcision** in the flesh made by hands; [13]**But now in Christ Jesus ye who sometimes were far off are made nigh** by the blood of Christ. [14]For he is our peace, who hath made **both one,** and hath **broken down the middle wall of partition between us;** [15]Having abolished in his flesh the enmity, even the law of commandments contained in ordinances; for to make in himself **of twain one new man,** so making peace; [16]And that he might reconcile **both** unto God in **one body by the cross,** having slain the enmity thereby: [17]And came and preached peace **to you which were afar off, and to them that were nigh.**

"The middle wall of partition between us" spoken of here was the barrier to keep Gentiles from entering the temple, *"between us."* Remember, Paul was accused of bringing a Gentile into the temple.

> *Acts 21:28* Crying out, Men of Israel, help: This is the man, that teacheth all men every where against the people, and the law, and this place: and further **brought Greeks also into the temple,** and hath polluted this holy place.

With Christ's atonement, there is no difference between Jew and Gentile, *"preached peace to you which were afar off, and to them that were nigh."* Gentiles were the people far off and Jews the ones that were nigh. How can there be a difference in the gospel?

> *Acts 15:8-9* And God, which knoweth the hearts, bare them witness, **giving them the Holy Ghost, even as he did unto us**; [9]And **put no difference between us and them**, purifying their hearts **by faith**.

> *Romans 3:22* Even the righteousness of God which is by faith of Jesus Christ **unto all and upon all them that believe: for there is no difference**:

> *Romans 10:11-12* For the scripture saith, Whosoever believeth on him shall not be ashamed. [12]**For there is no difference between the Jew and the Greek**: for the same Lord over all is rich unto all that call upon him.

> *Colossians 3:11* Where there is neither Greek nor Jew, circumcision nor uncircumcision, Barbarian, Scythian, bond nor free: but **Christ is all, and in all**.

There is no difference between Jew and Gentile!! How then can there be two gospels?? *"Put no difference between us and them, purifying their hearts by faith."* God was giving both, Jew and Gentile, the Holy Ghost and purifying their hearts by faith alone before Paul's conversion and ministry.

If you accept all of what Paul said, how can you possibly get two gospels? Paul contends that there is one gospel for both Jew and Gentile.

"Is Christ divided?" Who is causing the contention in the Church? Is it not those that say the gospel is divided, that they are of Paul and the Jews are of Peter?

> *1 Corinthians 1:11-13* For it hath been declared unto me of you, my brethren, by them which are of the house of Chloe, that **there are contentions among you**. [12]Now this I say, that every one of you saith, **I am of Paul**; and **I of Apollos**; and **I of Cephas**; and **I of Christ**. [13]**Is Christ divided?** was Paul crucified for you? or were ye baptized in the name of Paul?

> *1 Corinthians 3:4* For while one saith, **I am of Paul**; and another, I am of Apollos; **are ye not carnal**?

It is carnal Christians dividing Christ by saying I am of Paul and the Jews are of Peter.

Romans chapter 15 is an excellent exhortation of the unity of the Jew and Gentile Church and the one gospel Paul preached. In it, there is the gospel of God, the gospel of Christ, and the gospel, all synonymous with one another—verses 16, 19, 20, and 29.

Romans 15:16: That I should be the minister of Jesus Christ to the Gentiles, ministering **the gospel of God,**

Romans 15:19: I have fully preached **the gospel of Christ.**

Romans 15:20 Yea, so have I strived to preach **the gospel**

Romans 15:29: I shall come in the fulness of the blessing of **the gospel of Christ.**

These gospels are surely synonymous with these:

Ephesians 1:13: **the gospel of your salvation:**

Ephesians 6:15: **the gospel of peace;**

2 Thessalonians 1:8: **the gospel of our Lord Jesus Christ:**

Acts 20:24: **the gospel of the grace of God.**

Surely, these are the same gospel, the same one that was to be preached to all nations and every creature.

Mark 13:10 And **the gospel** must first be published among **all nations.**

Mark 16:15 And he said unto them, Go ye into all the world, and **preach the gospel to every creature.**

In our list at the beginning of this chapter, the gospel of the kingdom seems to be the only gospel that is not dealing with individual salvation but the restoration of the nation and kingdom of Israel.

Never in all of Paul's writings does he condone, advocate, not preach against there being any other gospel but the one he preached to both Jew and Gentile.

Galatians 1:8-9 But though we, or an angel from heaven, **preach any other gospel unto you than that which we have preached unto you, let him be accursed.** [9]As we said before, so say I now again, **If any man preach any other gospel unto you than that ye have received, let him be accursed.**

Paul testifies in no uncertain terms that there is but one gospel, the one he preached to both Jew and Gentile alike.

Works

And enter not into judgment with thy servant: for in thy sight shall no man living be justified.

—PSALM 143:2

A major problem for Grace Theology in teaching two gospels of salvation, one for the Jews and one for the Gentiles, is establishing what is the difference between them? There is only one name under heaven given whereby men must be saved. He gave himself once for all; not willing that any should perish, there is but one Holy Spirit which all receive. These are all particulars of Paul's gospel. To make two different gospels something must be added or taken away from this.

What do they have that they can take away from Paul's gospel, the Lord, the Holy Spirit, the one sacrifice? There is nothing that can be removed. This leaves adding something to Paul's gospel. What do they have they can add to make them different?

The only thing that can be changed is a different condition on which to receive salvation. The condition to receive the grace of God in Paul's gospel is believing, faith in the Lord Jesus Christ.

> *Ephesians 2:8-9* For **by grace** are ye saved **through faith**; and that **not of yourselves**: it is the gift of God: [9]**Not of works**, lest any man should boast.

It can be seen in the above verse that faith is contrasted against works. Works were briefly mentioned in the previous chapter. It is now necessary to go into more depth and detail.

Is it possible that Grace Theology is relying on the common misconception of the book of James and believe that "for by grace are ye save through **faith and works**; **it is partly** of yourselves **and partly** the gift of God"?

It matters not that some teaching Grace Theology do not admit to teaching works as necessary for the Jews, work is the only thing they can add to make the gospels different. Having spoken to many individuals advocating this teaching all ardently confessed before the atonement salvation was by works as well as it will be in the Tribulation. Whether aided by the misreading of James or not works is what they add to the gospel to make it different than Paul's holding to the concept that God's grace was only in one dispensation given to Paul.

Is it possible to be saved by grace and works? Is it possible to be saved by faith and works? Is it possible to be saved by works alone? These are the question that must be answered.

> *Romans 4:4* Now to him that worketh is the reward not reckoned of grace, **but of debt**.

Romans 4:16 Therefore **it is of faith, that it might be by grace**;

Regardless of what period of time you are speaking of, the above two verses and the precept they contain will apply, if by works it is not of grace or faith. If you are graciously given a free gift only to find a payment book with it, it is not free or a gift. Therefore, for Grace Theologies gospel to the Jews to be by works, it must remove grace and faith, "for ye Jews are saved through works; it is of yourselves: not the gift of God, not by grace". Would that statement fit anywhere within the Scriptures?

Keep this thought in mind when trying to interpret Galatians 2:7-9. Is the gospel of the circumcision one of works and the gospel of the uncircumcision one of grace?

Galatians 3:8 And the scripture, foreseeing that God would justify **the heathen through faith**, preached before **the gospel unto Abraham**, saying, In thee shall all nations be blessed.

Romans 4:13 For the promise, that he should be the heir of the world, **was not** to Abraham, or to his seed, **through the law, but through the righteousness of faith**.

The gospel is *"saved by grace through faith"* at all times, to all peoples. The Lord, Peter, James, John, Matthew, Luke, et al., preached the same gospel as Paul, Barnabas, Mark, Silas, etc. This is affirmed in Acts 15 at the great apostolic council where Peter, John, James, Paul, and many others, concluded that keeping the law was not necessary for Jew or Gentile to be saved.

Acts 15:10 Now therefore **why tempt ye God**, to put a yoke upon the neck of the disciples, **which neither our fathers nor we** were able to bear?

Acts 15:11 But **we believe** that through **the grace** of the Lord Jesus Christ **we shall be saved, even as they**.

We—the Jews; Peter, James, John, Paul, et al—believed that they were saved the same way as the Gentiles: *"through the grace of the Lord Jesus Christ."*

Salvation at any time, pre-crucifixion, post-crucifixion, Tribulation, is by grace through faith, not of works. Noah and Abraham, being examples, show it is a universal precept of God's word and not just a Pauline teaching, but the revelation of the mystery revealed to him.

Genesis 6:8 But **Noah found grace** in the eyes of the LORD.

Exodus 33:17 And **the LORD said unto Moses,** I will do this thing also that thou hast spoken: for **thou hast found grace in my sight,** and I know thee by name.

Romans 4:16 Therefore **it is of faith, that it might be by grace**;

Romans 11:6 And **if by grace, then is it no more of works**:

This is not difficult to explain. If salvation were by works anyone obtaining it would be glorifying himself, not God.

Ephesians 2:9 Not of works, **lest any man should boast**.

1 Corinthians 1:29 That **no flesh should glory in his presence**.

We are here to glorify God, not boast ourselves.

Grace Theology will go so far as to teach that Paul was the first person saved by grace through faith without works and the first to be in Christ, in the body. However, Paul preached the same faith he once destroyed and states that others were in Christ before him.

> *Galatians 1:23* But they had heard only, That he which **persecuted us** in times past **now preacheth the faith which once he destroyed**.

> *Romans 16:7* Salute Andronicus and Junia, my kinsmen, and my fellowprisoners, who are of note among the apostles, **who also were in Christ before me**.

It was the same faith, same gospel that Paul preached that he once persecuted. This shows that the gospel Paul preached was being preached before he was converted. Paul's gospel was not new, not a mystery hidden until revealed to him, but the same faith, same gospel, he had been persecuting.

In Galatians chapter 2, Paul is speaking to both Jew and Gentile, especially to Peter, when he confirms there is but one gospel and it is not one of works.

> *Galatians 2:21* I do not frustrate the grace of God: for **if righteousness come by the law, then Christ is dead in vain**.

Paul was speaking for all Jewish believers, even those in Christ before him, and he was certainly speaking to Peter when he said, *"Even we have believed in Jesus Christ, that we might be justified by the faith of Christ, and not by the works of the law: for **by the works of the law shall no flesh be justified**."*

At this point ask yourself, are the gospels of the circumcision and uncircumcision two different gospels, one by God's grace through our faith and one by our works, or is it one gospel and two different ministries?

"Not of works" is a universal biblical precept, not just a church age, dispensational, or Pauline teaching. Eternal salvation is never by works, alone or in concert with grace. Any teaching to the contrary is not biblical, not Christian doctrine. Unless this precept is accepted you will error in the formation of doctrine and teachings as Grace Theology has. [12]

---

[12] See "Methodology of Salvation," pg. 92 and "Dispensational Salvation," pg. 102 for further information on salvation's free gift.

Romans 4:14 For if they which are of the law be heirs, **faith is made void, and the promise made of none effect**:

Romans 11:6 And **if by grace, then is it no more of works**: otherwise grace is no more grace. But **if it be of works, then is it no more grace**: otherwise work is no more work.

A major stumbling block to their thinking is understanding biblical works. The Bible defines works as the keeping of God's law to establish self-righteousness, whether you are observing the given written statutes or verbal statutes of God. Remember, keeping the law of God is fulfilled in one commandment, *"love thy neighbour as thyself."* Violating the law is doing something to someone you would not want to be done to you.

Romans 13:9 For this, Thou shalt not commit adultery, Thou shalt not kill, Thou shalt not steal, Thou shalt not bear false witness, Thou shalt not covet; **and if there be any other commandment**, it is briefly comprehended in this saying, namely, **Thou shalt love thy neighbour as thyself.**

Galatians 5:14 For all the law is fulfilled in one word, even in this; Thou shalt love thy neighbour as thyself.

Noah building the Ark was not a work of obeying the law, it was an act of faith; *"it is of faith, that it might be by grace."* Abraham sacrificing his son was not a work of obeying the law; it was a trial of his faith.

Genesis 6:8 But Noah **found grace** in the eyes of the LORD.

1 Peter 1:7 That **the trial of your faith**, being much more precious than of gold that perisheth, **though it be tried** with fire, might be found unto praise and honour and glory at the appearing of Jesus Christ:

Hebrews 11:17 By faith **Abraham**, when **he was tried**, offered up Isaac: and he that had received the promises offered up his only begotten son,

Being told to do something by God is not the same as doing the works of the law given by God. Being baptized for the remission of sins is not a work of the law, not a work—period. It was a witness of the faith put in God's word that was being preached. It was also God's judgment and a snare on those that would not put their faith in his word.

Mark 11:30-32 The baptism of John, was it from heaven, or of men? answer me. [31]And they reasoned with themselves, saying, **If we shall say, From heaven; he will say, Why then did ye not believe him?** [32]But **if we shall say, Of men; they feared the people**: for all men counted John, that he was a prophet indeed.

Baptism is not a work. If someone had just followed the group and had been baptized by John, would they have received remission of sins—no. John's baptism was not only not a work—it was not salvation.

Acts 19:4 Then said Paul, John verily baptized with the **baptism of repentance, saying unto the people, that they should believe on him which should come after him**, that is, **on Christ Jesus**.

Even keeping the whole law of God without the right attitude and understanding, by faith, profited and obtained you nothing.

Romans 9:31-32 But Israel, which followed after the law of righteousness**, hath not attained to the law of righteousness.** [32]Wherefore? **Because <u>they sought it not by faith</u>, but as it were by the works of the law.** For **they stumbled at that stumblingstone**;

"If by grace, then is it no more of works." "It is of faith, that it might be by grace." If it is by grace, there is no element of works. It is either works or grace; God will not accept any man's works. He will accept the faith if that is what provoked and caused the works.

Hebrews 11:6 But **without faith it is impossible to please him**:

Romans 4:16 Therefore **it is of faith, that it might be by grace**;

Romans 11:6 And **if by grace, then is it no more of works:** ... **if it be of works, then is it no more grace**:

Hebrews chapter 11 is filled with the examples of Old Testament saints and their faith toward God: *"it is of faith, that it might be by grace."* It is their faith that found them grace in God's eyes, not their works. It was their faith that caused them to do the works, the works that proved they had faith.

It is not faith and works
It is not faith or works
It is faith that works

Dispensations

If ye have heard of the dispensation of the grace of God which is given me to you-ward:

—EPHESIANS 3:2

Dispensational teaching is the dividing of the Bible into divisions of time or ages. The usual divisions are:

1. **Innocence**—Adam and Eve before they sinned

2. **Conscience**—first sin to the flood

3. **Civil Government**—after the flood

4. **Promise**—Abraham to Moses, the Law is given

5. **Law**—Moses to the cross

6. **Church or Grace**—cross to the millennial kingdom

7. **Millennial Kingdom**—the rule of Christ on earth

Dispensational charts are formed in several ways with different numbered divisions. The above list would be considered a common chart and manner of explaining dispensations. Regardless of what religious belief system sets forth their idea of dispensations, there is one very grave mistake associated with many including ones use by Grace Theology. That error is assigning salvation by grace as existing in just one dispensation.

The one called the Church dispensation is also known by some as the dispensation of grace with the specific meaning that it is only in this dispensation that men are saved by grace through faith and not of works. The rest having an element of works; it has been seen in the previous chapter this is not consistent with the Scriptures.

Salvation at any time is by the grace of God to the exclusion of any and all works and never by any other way.

> *Romans 11:5-6* Even so then at this present time also there is a remnant **according to the election of grace**. ⁶And **if by grace, then is it no more of works**: otherwise grace is no more grace. But **if it be of works, then is it no more grace**: otherwise work is no more work.

All dispensations, however differently God was dealing with men, are all a dispensation of God's grace: grace = faith without works.

> *Romans 4:16* Therefore **it is of faith, that it might be by grace**;

Part of Grace Theology's mistake is going by this mistaken belief that the grace of God is covered by just one dispensation. Grace Theology is also known as Hyper-Dispensationalism due to their teaching that Paul was given the dispensation of grace with a different gospel to go with it.

This too is derived by taking things out of context and not diligently comparing scripture with scripture. Paul was not given **THE** dispensation; he was given **A** dispensation.

> *1 Corinthians 9:17* For if I do this thing willingly, I have a reward: but if against my will, **a dispensation of the gospel** is committed unto me.

Paul was given *"**a** dispensation of the gospel,"* which, according to him, was a dispensation of the grace of God.

> *Ephesians 3:2* If ye have heard of **the dispensation of the grace** of God which is given me to you-ward:

If I give you **A** pencil, then you have **THE** pencil I gave you, and you can say, "See **THE** pencil which was given to me." But it is still **A** pencil, one of many.

So here is one gospel separated into several dispensations, *"a dispensation of the gospel."* The dispensation Paul was given was one dispensation of the same gospel as other dispensations. All the dispensations are dispensations of God's grace.

> *Colossians 1:25* Whereof I am made a minister, according to **the dispensation of God** which is **given to me for you**, to fulfil the word of God;

The dispensation he was given was *"a dispensation of the gospel."* Paul was given a ministry, a dispensation of the gospel of the grace of God to the Gentiles. It was not a different gospel but a different ministry, the ministry of the grace of God to the heathen, those that had not the law.

> *Romans 2:14* For when the Gentiles, **which have not the law,**

Why would it be that Paul was given the ministry to the Gentiles and not Peter? Could it be that the Gentiles, *"which have not the law,"* would not benefit from the law as a schoolmaster to bring them unto Christ?

> *Galatians 3:24* Wherefore **the law was our schoolmaster to bring us unto Christ**, that we might be justified by faith.

Possibly the ministry needed someone to explain the law and its purpose to them, a doctor of the law: Saul of Tarsus, J.D., graduate of the school of Gamaliel, taught according to the perfect manner of the law of the fathers.

> *1 Corinthians 9:8* Say I these things as a man? or **saith not the law the same also**?

It could be the Gentiles required a little tutelage so that they would not be deceived by another or perverted gospel.

> *Galatians 3:12* And **the law is not of faith**:

146

Galatians 3:28 There is neither Jew nor Greek, there is neither bond nor free, there is neither male nor female: **for ye are all one in Christ Jesus**.

In order to kick start the Gentiles, they needed instruction in the law for several reasons. It was necessary to know from what they needed to be saved, how they were supposed to live, and the knowledge of the prophecies contained within the law to strengthen their faith. Hence, a dispensation of the gospel was given to Dr. Paul, Attorney-at-Law. It was not a different gospel but a special ministry.

Mysteries

Let a man so account of us, as of the ministers of Christ, and stewards of the mysteries of God.

—1 CORINTHIANS 4:1

Grace Theology teaches that salvation by grace through faith was a mystery given to Paul by virtue of being given the dispensation of grace. The dispensations were covered in the last chapter, in this one, the mysteries in the Bible will be look at.

The mystery of the faith is God being manifested in the flesh, that God was in Christ:

> *1 Timothy 3:9-16* Holding **the mystery of the faith** in a pure conscience.... [16]And without controversy great is **the mystery of godliness**: **God was manifest in the flesh,...**

> *2 Corinthians 5:18-19* And all things are of God, who hath reconciled us to himself by Jesus Christ, and hath given to us the ministry of reconciliation; [19]To wit, that **God was in Christ, reconciling the world unto himself**, not imputing their trespasses unto them; and hath committed unto us the word of reconciliation.

> *Colossians 2:2-3* That their hearts might be comforted, being knit together in love, and unto all riches of the full assurance of understanding, to the acknowledgement of **the mystery of God, and of the Father, and of Christ**; [3]In whom are hid all the treasures of wisdom and knowledge.

> *John 10:30* **I and my Father are one**.

> *John 14:10* Believest thou not that **I am in the Father, and the Father in me?** the words that I speak unto you I speak not of myself: but **the Father that dwelleth in me**, he doeth the works.

The mystery that Christ is in the believer,

> *John 14:20* At that day ye shall know that **I am in my Father**, and **ye in me, and I in you**.

> *Colossians 1:26* Even **the mystery** ... which is **Christ in you, the hope of glory**:

Is Christ teaching anything different than Paul?

Futher, the mystery that the Church is Christ's body.

> *Ephesians 5:30-32* For we are members of his body, of his flesh, and of his bones.... [32]**This is a great mystery: but I speak concerning Christ and the church**.

That the Gentiles are fellow heirs and of the same body with the Jews,

148

Ephesians 3:3-6 How that **by revelation** he made known unto me **the mystery**; ... ⁶That **the Gentiles should be fellowheirs, and of the same body, and partakers of his promise in Christ by the gospel**:

And the mystery that the saved will be changed from mortality to immortality:

1 Corinthians 15:51-55 Behold, **I shew you a mystery**; We shall not all sleep, **but we shall all be changed**, ... the dead **shall be raised incorruptible**, and **we shall be changed**....

Matthew 22:30 For **in the resurrection they** neither marry, nor are given in marriage, but **are as the angels of God in heaven**.

Is Christ teaching anything different than Paul?

In addition to the mysteries related to the faith, there are a couple of others: the mystery of all things being gathered together in Christ:

Ephesians 1:9-10 Having made known unto us the mystery of his will, ... ¹⁰That in the dispensation of the fulness of times **he might gather together in one all things in Christ, both which are in heaven, and which are on earth; even in him**:

Colossians 2:2-3 That their hearts might be comforted, being knit together in love, and unto all riches of the full assurance of understanding, to the acknowledgement of **the mystery of God, and of the Father, and of Christ**; ³In whom are hid all the treasures of wisdom and knowledge.

The mystery of Israel not being cast off but blinded for a time:

Romans 11:25 For I would not, brethren, that ye should be ignorant of this mystery, ... that **blindness in part is happened to Israel, until the fulness of the Gentiles be come in**.

The mystery of the kingdom of God:

Mark 4:11 And he said unto them, Unto you it is given to know **the mystery of the kingdom of God**: but unto them that are without, all these things are done in parables:

The mystery of the seven stars and candlesticks:

Revelation 1:20 **The mystery of the seven stars** which thou sawest in my right hand, **and the seven golden candlesticks.** The seven stars are the angels of the seven churches: and the seven candlesticks which thou sawest are the seven churches.

The mystery of Babylon the Great:

Revelation 17:5 And upon her forehead was a name written, **MYSTERY, BABYLON THE GREAT**, THE MOTHER OF HARLOTS AND ABOMINATIONS OF THE EARTH.

These are the mysteries of the Bible. Take note that there is no mystery of salvation by grace through faith. The gospel of salvation by the grace of God through our faith in him is a universal precept of the Scriptures. God will not allow any man to stand before him and declare his own righteousness by his own works at any time.

> *Isaiah 64:6* But **we are all as an unclean thing**, and **all our righteousnesses are as filthy rags**; and we all do fade as a leaf; and our iniquities, like the wind, have taken us away.

In Closing

Now this I say, that every one of you saith, I am of Paul; and I of Apollos; and I of Cephas; and I of Christ.

—1 CORINTHIANS 1:12

It has been seen that Paul was given *"a dispensation of the gospel,"* which as all dispensations, are *"the dispensation of the grace of God"* given to him to minister to the Gentiles. Paul was the foremost defender of there being but one gospel, one faith, with no difference between Jew and Gentile.

It has been shown that there is nothing that can be taken away from Paul's gospel to make it different than Peter's. Further, if works are added it nullified grace and faith, nullifying the gospel.

> *Job 25:4* **How then can man be justified with God?** or **how can he be clean that is born of a woman**?

> *Romans 4:14* For if they which are of the law be heirs, **faith is made void, and the promise made of none effect**:

> *Galatians 2:21* I do not frustrate the grace of God: for **if righteousness come by the law, then Christ is dead in vain.**

Paul most assuredly did not preach a divided Church, a dual gospel.

> *Ephesians 4:4-6* There is **one body**, and **one Spirit**, even as ye are called in **one hope** of your calling; [5]**One Lord, one faith, one baptism**, [6]**One God** and Father of all, who is above all, and through all, and in you all.

Paul preached one undivided gospel and a curse on anyone who preached another. Grace Theology is divisive in that they preach two gospels say the Gentiles are of Paul and the Jews are of Peter.

> *1 Corinthians 1:23-24* But **we preach Christ crucified, unto the Jews** a stumblingblock, and **unto the Greeks** foolishness; [24]But unto them which are called, **both Jews and Greeks**, Christ the power of God, and the wisdom of God.

> *Romans 15:16* That I should be **the minister of Jesus Christ to the Gentiles**, ministering **the gospel of God**, that the offering up of the Gentiles might be acceptable, being sanctified by the Holy Ghost.

"Ministering the gospel of God" to the Gentiles, not ministering the gospel of the Gentiles, the gospel of the uncircumcision to the uncircumcision.

> *Galatians 1:8-9* But **though we, or an angel from heaven, preach any other gospel unto you than that which we have preached unto you, let him be accursed**. [9]As we said before, so

say I now again, **If any man preach any other gospel unto you than that ye have received, let him be accursed**.

It has never been by the act of doing what God said to obtain righteousness but by doing it out of faith toward him. Salvation has always been and always will be by God's grace through faith in him, which excludes works of any kind.

Romans 4:4 Now to him that worketh is the reward **not reckoned of grace, but of debt**.

It seems apparent that Grace Theology has not completely made it over the *"stumblingstone."*

Job 19:25 For I know that **my redeemer liveth**, and that he shall stand at the latter day upon the earth:

Paul was given *"a dispensation of the gospel," "the gospel of the grace of God,"* not a unique dispensation particular to Gentiles.

1 Corinthians 9:17 For if I do this thing willingly, I have a reward: but if against my will, **a dispensation of the gospel** is committed unto me.

It was just one of several dispensations of the gospel. It has always been a gospel of grace that was divided into dispensations, grace throughout all dispensations. Salvation by the gospel of grace through faith was not a mystery solely given to Paul. Granted, Noah, Job, Abraham, and the Old Testament saints might not have known that their salvation was contingent upon the death, burial, and resurrection of Christ Jesus for the payment of sins, but it was upon their faith that God granted them his grace and forgiveness of sins.[13]

Paul ministered to both Jew and Gentile. After his pronouncement of a curse on any other gospel, I doubt he preached a different one to the Jews.

Romans 15:25 But now **I go unto Jerusalem to minister unto the saints**.

Just as importantly, the mysteries were not only revealed to Paul but to others as well.

Ephesians 3:4-5 Whereby, when ye read, ye may understand my knowledge in the mystery of Christ) [5]Which in other ages was not made known unto the sons of men, as **it is now revealed unto his holy apostles and prophets** by the Spirit;

Taking all that has been said into consideration, how can it be asserted that there is more than one gospel of the saving grace of God through faith in the Lord Jesus Christ? There is only one other gospel in the

---

[13]See "Methodology of Salvation," pg 92 and "Dispensational Salvation," pg 102.

Scriptures and that is the gospel of the kingdom which concerns Israel as a nation and the restoration of its kingdom in the millennium.

The consequences of this error might not be clearly seen at this time, but it is a false understanding of God's word. As such it can only bring harm to the gospel of salvation if only by the confusion and division it causes within the Church of God. Where this theology began is inconsequential; diligent study and rightly dividing God's word is all that is needed to understand that it is in error.

All of what has been said in this study must be considered and explained away for Grace Theology to maintain itself. Some of the brethren will stick to their guns no matter what, for many reasons, all bad. The one sure fact is that they reject half of what Paul, the apostle they claim as theirs, says. Then there are false brethren, false apostles, false prophets, false teachers, and Satan and his minions, bringing in damnable heresies. This is not a pointed condemnation of anyone, it is just a fact. Many advocating this doctrine have been soul winners. However, the many deceivers warned about is the reason each one of us needs to know and study the Bible for ourselves.

Peter preached grace through faith for salvation, the same as Paul.

1 Peter 1:9-10 Receiving the end of **your faith**, even the **salvation of your souls**. [10]Of which salvation the prophets have enquired and searched diligently, who **prophesied of the grace** that should come unto you:

Nothing less than a whole Bible can make a whole Christian.

—A.W. Tozer (1897-1963)
American Christian pastor, author

FAITH
OF
JESUS

INTRODUCTION

For there must be also heresies among you, that they which are approved may be made manifest among you.

—1 Corinthians 11:19

This study is a study on faith, what it is, and its relation to an error that is becoming more pervasive within the Church. An error that is a subtle, innocent-looking misinterpretation designed to convince that it is glorifying God when in fact it is corrupting his word.

The error is the misinterpretation of the following group of words.

- the faith of God

- the faith of Jesus Christ

- the faith of Christ,

These and other like phrases are being taken out of their context and a false meaning applied. They are interpreted to mean that it is God's faith or Jesu's faith and not our faith in them. They derive this private interpretation by violating one of the basic rules of *"rightly dividing the word of truth."*

A sentence is the smallest unit of grammar that has a definite meaning. Any meaning can be applied to a clause, phrase, or group of words when removed from the context of their sentence.

A sentence is a trinity, it must have a subject, predicate (verb), and a complete thought. Anything less than a sentence lacks one of those three and has no definitive meaning.

This error often insinuates if not directly teaches that men are not capable of having faith, that it is a gift that must be given them by God, or more to the point, it is God's or Christ's faith that is given to us. This fallacy has been leavening the Church for centuries. Today the fruit of that leavening is evident in the error discussed in this study.

To begin a consideration of the biblical definition of faith in all its aspects is needed. The definition of faith may be well known to many, but due to the attacks on it, a refresher is not unreasonable. The errors covered here are far from harmless; their unforeseen consequences are very destructive. I have seen firsthand a young family ill-equipped, weak in the faith, being pushed out to a supposed calling based on, "Not to worry, God will give you the faith to succeed," or "You are not going on your faith it is the Lord's faith that will sustain you." Unfortunately, the Lord's faith did not sustain nor was faith provided and a young family was destroyed, torn apart when the young man was overwhelmed, returning to the world losing his wife and children.

There should be no doubt that if Satan can destroy one family with this deception many others have or will be also. This teaching is a pernicious falsehood with devastating repercussions, and it has been seeping into the thinking of many Bible teachers who are not diligently studying it out.

Galatians 5:9 **A little leaven leaveneth the whole lump**.

Make the word of God as much as possible its own interpreter. You will best understand the word of God by comparing it with itself. *"Comparing spiritual things with spiritual"*

Sir Isaac Newton (1642-1727)
English Physicist & Mathematician

Definition

But without faith it is impossible to please him: for he that cometh to God must believe that he is, and that he is a rewarder of them that diligently seek him.

—HEBREWS 11:6

God has elected that faith is a determining factor as to whether or not we *"please him."* Few of the disputes and controversies debated within the Church are as important or as consequential as those embroiling faith. It is required of us to be pleasing to God, essential for salvation, and its absence in anything constitutes sin.

Romans 14:23 for **whatsoever is not of faith is sin**.

For these reasons, understanding what the Scriptures mean by it would be advisable.

The definition of *"faith,"* or rather the perceived definition, is itself a stumbling block and has been for centuries. It is often added to and occasionally considered to be a mystical quality beyond man's ability to have.

> Faith is a divine virtue that can only occur in the human breast by an act of divine grace.
>
> Thomas Aquinas (1225-1274)

> Faith is the gift of God's grace; it is not merited, earned, nor self-created.
>
> Emil Brunner (1899-1966)

But, what does the Scriptures have to say?

As this is a word study it would be proper to begin by simply looking at the dictionary definition of faith. Most abridged dictionaries will give the two most common meanings.

Faith:

1. Confidence, reliance, trust; belief
2. That which is believed or the object of belief

The two meanings simply look at faith from opposite ends.

- I have faith in this—this is my faith
- I have faith in Jesus Christ—I hold to the faith of Jesus Christ

Revelation 14:12 Here is the patience of the saints: here are they **that keep** the commandments of God, and **the faith of Jesus**.

158

"That keep ... the faith of Jesus." The fact that faith can be looked at from these two directions will be an especially important concept to remember in studying this error. Two examples of it being used for the objects of belief are found in Galatians and 1 Timothy.

Galatians 1:23 But they had heard only, That he which persecuted us in times past now preacheth **the faith** which once he destroyed.

1 Timothy 3:9 Holding the mystery of **the faith** in a pure conscience.

"The faith" in these verses stands for the corporate beliefs or objects of the belief that Paul once persecuted but now preaches. He persecuted those who held faith in Jesus Christ; he persecuted *"the faith of Jesus Christ."* Thankfully, he now holds *"the faith of Jesus Christ."*

The biblical definition of faith is also to believe.

Hebrews 11:6 But **without faith** it is impossible to please him: for he that cometh to God **must believe** that he is,...

"Faith ... must believe," having the faith needed to please God begins with believing he is.

Isaiah 43:10 Ye are my witnesses, saith the LORD, and my servant whom I have chosen: that ye may know and **believe me**, and understand that **I am he:** before me there was no God formed, neither shall there be after me.

The Lord has always been attempting to get men to believe, put their faith, in him.

Numbers 14:11 And the LORD said unto Moses, How long will this people provoke me? and how long will it be **ere they believe me**, for all the signs which I have showed among them?

Deuteronomy 32:20 And he said, I will hide my face from them, I will see what their end shall be: for they are a very froward generation, children **in whom is no faith**.

Faith is also defined in Romans as believing.

Romans 4:3-5 For what saith the scripture? Abraham **believed God**, and **it was counted unto him for righteousness**. [4]Now to him that worketh is the reward not reckoned of grace, but of debt. [5]But to him that worketh not, but **believeth** on him that justifieth the ungodly, **his faith is counted for righteousness**.

It is God who justifies the ungodly. Believing on him is defined in the above passage as exercising one's own faith, *"his faith is counted for righteousness."* Take note here that faith/belief is in contrast to works: *"to him that* ***worketh not, but believeth."***

Romans 4:16 Therefore **it is of faith, that it might be by grace**; to the end the promise might be sure to all the seed; not to that only which is of the law, but to that also which is of **the faith of Abraham**; who is the father of us all,

Is the above verse speaking of Abraham's faith being given to us or is it that we have the same faith that Abraham had?

The Lord was consistently faulting men for not having faith.

Matthew 6:30: O **ye of little faith**?

Matthew 8:26: Why are ye fearful, **O ye of little faith**?

Matthew 14:31: **O thou of little faith**, wherefore didst thou doubt?

Matthew 16:8: O **ye of little faith**,

Luke 12:28: O **ye of little faith**?

Matthew 21:25: **Why did ye not then believe him**?

Mark 4:40: **how is it that ye have no faith**?

Mark 5:36: Be not afraid, **only believe**.

Mark 9:23: **If thou canst believe**, all things are possible **to him that believeth**.

The point being, how can men be reproved of the Lord for not having something that they must obtain as a gift from him?

Many times, Ephesians 2:8-9 is used to support the teaching that faith is a gift from God, and it is a good example of how the lack of applying the principles of basic grammar can lead to false interpretations.

Ephesians 2:8-9 For by grace are ye saved through faith; and that not of yourselves: **it is the gift of God**: [9]Not of works, lest any man should boast.

These two verses contain one compound sentence which by definition means it is two or more independent sentences put together to show a closer relationship. If proper grammar is adhered to the clarity of its correct interpretation will be obtained. First, divide the compound sentence into its independent sentences.

For by grace are ye saved through faith; and that not of yourselves.

It is the gift of God: Not of works, lest any man should boast.

Now to find the simple sentences and its real complete thought, remove all the modifiers and conjunctions, adjectives, adverbs, etc. This leaves us the two simple sentences.

Ye are saved. It is the gift.

In the first sentence, *"through faith"* as well as *"by grace,"* and *"not of yourselves,"* are prepositional adverbial phrases and are treated as one-word adverbs. They all modify the verb *"are."* Being used in an adverb

160

phrase, the noun faith is not the antecedent to any pronoun; faith is not the gift. The noun *"saved"* is the antecedent to *"it."*

Prepositional phrases show relationships, on the table, under the table, etc. There are three relationships: "by grace" *"through faith"* and *"not of yourselves."* The antecedent of *"it"* is the noun *"saved,"* not the noun *"faith"* which is being used as an adverb in an adverbial phrase.

Ye are saved. It (saved) is the gift of God.

Understanding and applying basic grammar can be tedious but it is indispensable in rightly dividing the word of truth. By not doing so, a phrase or group of words can be said to mean anything. Salvation is the gift of God's grace, not faith. Salvation is granted to an individual through his faith in the gospel of Christ Jesus. Putting your faith in Christ Jesus is the requirement, the condition, to receive the gift of salvation. Salvation is conditional, contingent on our faith.

In determining biblically that faith is synonymous with believing, it must also be realized that believing is not necessarily faith.

> *John 20:29* Jesus saith unto him, Thomas, because **thou hast seen** me, **thou hast believed**: blessed are they **that have not seen**, and **yet have believed**.

You can believe something because you have seen and touched, *"because thou hast seen me, thou hast believed,"* or by faith, *"blessed are they that have not seen, and yet have believed."* This is a general principle, a precept, of the Scriptures that was most succinctly expressed by Blaise Pascal in the mid-1600s.

> God has determined that divine things should enter through the heart into the mind, and not through the mind into the heart. In divine things, therefore, it is necessary to love them in order to know them.[14]
>
> Blaise Pascal (1623-1662) French Mathematician, Physicist, Theologian

God has chosen to believe by faith, not through knowledge and understanding. This is a general precept of God's word. It explains why atheists, evolutionists, and the like do not see and understand creation the same as men of faith. God will not allow it to be seen and understood even when that understanding would lead to believing in him or in his word. You must believe in him and his word first.

> *Acts 9:18* And **immediately there fell from his eyes as it had been scales**: and he received sight forthwith, and arose, and was baptized.

It is common for some to mistakenly assume God is preventing men from believing his word in verses such as the following:

---

[14]Blaise Pascal 1623~62; French Mathematician, Physicist, Theologian

Acts 28:26 Saying, Go unto this people, and say, **Hearing ye shall hear, and shall not understand; and seeing ye shall see, and not perceive**:

Matthew 13:14 And in them is fulfilled the prophecy of Esaias, which saith, **By hearing ye shall hear, and shall not understand; and seeing ye shall see, and shall not perceive**:

Mark 4:12 That seeing they may see, and not perceive; and hearing they may hear, and not understand; **lest at any time they should be converted, and their sins should be forgiven them.**

God is not preventing them from believing by faith from the heart, he is preventing them from understanding and believing from the head. He has chosen faith, to trust in him, even when you do not understand. To put it another way, God will not settle for wisdom and understanding gained leading to the discovery of him; wisdom and understanding must begin with and flow from him through faith in him. The eyes of faith see things a bit differently than those of unbelief.

Men have faith in almost everything they normally do. Without faith, you are a psychotic paranoid personality. Men have faith that they can drive headlong at each other with only a four-inch painted line to keep them from crashing. A door could not be opened without faith that there was nothing on the other side that was going to hurt us. The Bible uses the word *"faith"* in one sense, in reference to one thing and one thing only: *"faith toward God."* Faith toward God, faith toward the Lord Jesus Christ, is its only biblical use.

Hebrews 6:1 Therefore leaving **the principles of the doctrine of Christ**, let us go on unto perfection; not laying again the foundation of repentance from dead works, and of **faith toward God**, Of the doctrine of baptisms, and of laying on of hands, and of resurrection of the dead, and of eternal judgment.

Acts 20:21 Testifying both to the Jews, and also to the Greeks, repentance toward God, and **faith toward our Lord Jesus Christ**.

It ought to be evident at this point, seeing that faith is synonymous with believing, biblically it is about *"faith toward God"* only. It is each and every one of us that have to rouse that faith from within us. Believing/faith is not a gift, it is required of us.

This understanding of the biblical definition of faith can be used to study and judge the correctness of the interpretations at issue, the errors that provoked this study.

Meditate on These Things

Meditate upon these things; give thyself wholly to them; that thy profiting may appear to all.
—*1 TIMOTHY 4:15*

The error being opposed is the teaching that phrases as the following represent God's or Jesus Christ's faith and not our faith in them.

Romans 3:3: the **faith of God**...

Romans 3:22: by **faith of Jesus Christ**

Revelation 14:12: the **faith of Jesus**.

Before looking at the context and begin diagramming sentences there is one more aspect of our *"faith toward God"* and Christ to explore.

Hebrews 11:1 Now **faith is the substance of things hoped for**, the **evidence of things not seen**.

We know from the previous chapter that Hebrews 11:1 is not the definition of faith, it is rather an effect of faith. It is our *"faith toward God"* that is the substance of things hoped for. It is our walking in the faith, living by the faith, that is an evident token of the things unseen.

Philippians 1:27-28 Only let your conversation **be as it becometh the gospel of Christ**: that whether I come and see you, or else be absent, I may hear of your affairs, that **ye stand fast in one spirit, with one mind striving together for the faith of the gospel**; [28]And **in nothing terrified by your adversaries**: which is to them **an evident token of perdition**, but **to you of salvation**, and that of God.

Our living our faith condemns the lost, that is why they hate us. Our being steadfast in the faith is a witness of the truth and the evidence of their own destruction. Our *"faith toward God"* is a testimony of the things we hope for, and the evidence of those things not seen as yet. Trusting God, believing his word, and obeying it is our works, without which we have no testimony of our hope and salvation. That is why our faith without those works is dead because it does not affect others.

James 2:17-18 Even so **faith, if it hath not works, is dead, being alone.** [18]Yea, a man may say, Thou hast faith, and I have works: shew me thy faith without thy works, and **I will shew thee my faith by my works.**

In light of this, the question must be asked; what is God going to put faith in? What does he have to hope for? He created all things, he sees all things, he knows all things. What is he going to have faith in? He is in control of all things!

163

We only see in part; we need faith.

2 Corinthians 5:7 (For **we walk by faith, not by sight:**)

1 Corinthians 13:12 For now we **see** through **a glass, darkly**; but then face to face: now **I know in part**; but then shall I know even as also I am known.

We cannot see it all thus we have to walk by faith. The contrast is faith opposed to sight.

Romans 8:24 For we are saved by hope: but hope that is seen is not hope: for **what a man seeth, why doth he yet hope for**?

God sees all; there is nothing for God to have faith in.

Psalms 139:12 Yea, the darkness hideth not from thee; but the night shineth as the day: the darkness and **the light are both alike to thee**.

Hebrews 4:13 Neither is there any creature that is not manifest in his sight: but **all things are naked and opened unto the eyes of him with whom we have to do**.

Proverbs 15:3 The eyes of the LORD are **in every place**, beholding the evil and the good.

Faith is not an attribute of God. So, without examining the context or diagramming a sentence, we know that the teaching that these phrases are to be interpreted as God having or exercising faith is in error. God does not walk by faith.

The next chapter will look at some of the references that are being misinterpreted and apply what has been shown as the biblical definition of faith to them. Below is a short review of what has been discussed up to this point.

1. Faith is believing.
2. The Bible uses faith in only one sense, believing God.
3. The Bible contrast faith against works.
4. The Bible contrast faith against seeing.
5. Faith is believing from the heart, not the head.

With these points confirmed and in our minds, it is time to approach the topic head-on.

Rightly Dividing

**Study to shew thyself approved unto God, a
workman that needeth not to be ashamed, rightly
dividing the word of truth.**

—2 TIMOTHY 2:15

Our first reference will be the phrase *"the faith of God,"* which in
actuality is just a group of words removed from the context of their sentence.

> *Romans 3:3* For what if some did not believe? shall their unbelief
> make **the faith of God** without effect?

To interpret this verse, you have to remember what was just stated in
the previous chapter. Chapter 2 is a discourse on believing and non-believing
Jews, keeping or not keeping the law, and that it will not affect
the judgments of God.

> *Romans 2:12-13* For as many as have sinned without law **shall
> also perish without law**: and as many as have sinned in the law
> **shall be judged by the law;** [13](For **not the hearers of the law are
> just before God**, but the **doers of the law shall be justified**.

Looking at verse 3 in light of chapter 2 it will be seen that it is a contrast
between belief and unbelief.

> *Romans 3:3* For what if some **did not believe**? shall their **unbelief**
> make **the faith of God** without effect?

It is asking if the unbelief of some in *"the oracles of God,"*—God's
word—will void the belief that others have.

> *Romans 3:2* Much every way: chiefly, because that unto them
> were committed **the oracles of God**.

Will their faith in God's word be useless or without effect because
someone else does not believe? The words *"faith of God"* here has the
same meaning as in Titus.

> Titus 1:1 Paul, a servant of God, and an apostle of Jesus Christ,
> according to **the faith of God's elect**, and the acknowledging of
> the truth which is after godliness;

Will the unbelief of some in God's word make void the faith/belief of
God's elect in his word? God forbid. In accordance with the definition
and use of the word *"faith"* in the Scriptures described in the previous
chapters and keeping with the context that this passage is found in, this
is the only interpretation that is biblically sound. To place any other interpretation
on those words is against every precept of *"rightly dividing
the word of truth."*

There are several other references to which this error is applied.

Galatians 2:20 **the faith of the Son of God**

Ephesians 3:12 **the faith of him**

James 2:1 **the faith of our Lord Jesus Christ**

Philippians 3:9 And be found in him, not having mine own righteousness, which is of the law, but that which is **through the faith of Christ**, the righteousness which is **of God by faith**:

The above verses should be interpreted the same as these below.

Romans 4:16 but to that also which is of **the faith of Abraham**; who is the father of us all,

Philippians 1:27 **the faith of the gospel**;

Colossians 2:12 **the faith of the operation of God**,

Is Abraham imputing faith to us, or is it our faith like Abraham's believing God? Is the gospel exercising faith, or is it our faith in the gospel? Does the operation of God have faith, or is it our faith in the operation? Clearly, this erroneous interpretation cannot be applied consistently and therefore must be suspect and rightfully questioned.

This false interpretation is often showcased with the use of Galatians 2:15-16. It is again the product of wrongly dividing the word of truth by taking the group of words *"the faith of Jesus Christ"* out of their context.

Look at Galatians 2:15-16; the two verses contain one sentence. It can be broken down without too much trouble.

Galatians 2:15-16 We who are Jews by nature, and not sinners of the Gentiles, [16]Knowing that a man is not justified by the works of the law, but by **the faith of Jesus Christ**, even **we have believed in Jesus Christ**, that we might be justified by **the faith of Christ**, and not by the works of the law: for by the works of the law shall no flesh be justified.

Here again, the only way to interpret the words *"the faith of Jesus Christ"* as Christ having faith is to take them out of the context of their sentence. By breaking this sentence down, taking all the modifiers out, we will be left with a simple sentence of a subject, verb, and the proper complete thought.

We who are Jews by nature, and not sinners of the Gentiles, Knowing that a man is not justified by the works of the law, but by the faith of Jesus Christ, even **we have believed** in Jesus Christ, that we might be justified by the faith of Christ, and not by the works of the law: for by the works of the law shall no flesh be justified.

Removing the modifiers leaves just the simple sentence of a subject being *"we"* and the verb *"have believed."* Diagramming the sentence is easy enough.

The complete thought of the sentence is that they, the Jews, have believed something, put their faith in something. The Jews are the doers of the action.

The rest of the sentence contained in these two verses are modifiers either modifying the subject *"we"*, the verb *"have believed,"* and adding to and explaining the complete thought of *"We have believed"* or we have put our faith in something. They are going to tell us who *"we"* are and what and why *"we"* are believing.

Adding the modifiers back in for the subject first, *"we"* is modified to explain exactly who *"we"* is:

We are Jews by nature

We are not sinners of the Gentiles

We are Knowing that a man is **justified**

    not by the **works**

        of the law

    but by the **faith**

        of Jesus Christ

We see then that the subject *"we"* of the sentence are natural-born Jews and not Gentile converts. Jews who are knowing that Justification is not in keeping the law but by faith.

The verb *"have believed"* is modified by:

We have believed

    in Jesus Christ

We have believed

    that we might be justified

        by the **faith**

            of Christ,

        not by the **works**

            of the law

We have the same phrasing as *"the faith of Jesus Christ"* in the phrase *"the works of the law."* Is it the works that the law is doing on our behalf, or is it the work *"We,"* the Jews, are doing in relation to the law? It is the works the Jews are doing in relation to the law. So, it is with faith; it is their faith in or in relation to Jesus Christ, not Christ's faith that justifies them. "In relation to" is a definition of "of," not by the works (in relation) to the law.

It is understandable that studying, especially grammar, can be tedious work. Understanding what the Bible says requires it.

Ecclesiastes 12:12 **much study is a weariness of the flesh**.

Another point that is good to remember is that verse numbers are not part of grammar and should not be considered in dividing and diagramming a sentence. They do serve an important role in aiding the study of the Scriptures in that they separate thoughts. A sentence has to have at least one complete thought but can have sub-thoughts combining to make that complete thought.

There are sentences in the New Testament that contain more than two hundred words (Colossians 1:21-29 as an example). These verses are often misread and misinterpreted. It may be a bit of effort to exercise proper grammar, but it is worth it to ensure you are correctly interpreting and understanding God's word.

> Proverbs 2:3-5 Yea, if thou **criest after knowledge**, and **liftest up thy voice for understanding**; [4]If thou **seekest her as silver**, and **searchest for her as for hid treasures**; [5]**Then shalt thou understand** the fear of the LORD, **and find the knowledge of God**.

God never meant for everything in the Scriptures to be easy to understand. He would like to see some effort on our parts, some desire, to know and understand him.

Final Thoughts

By faith Enoch was translated that he should not see death; and was not found, because God had translated him: for before his translation he had this testimony, that he pleased God.

—Hebrews 11:5

We are admonished throughout the whole Bible to believe in, on, and put our total trust, our faith, in God and our Saviour Jesus Christ. Hebrews chapter 11 gives examples of men and women who trusted in God to exhort us to walk in that same faith.

Hebrews 11:1-40 Now **faith is the substance of things hoped for,** the evidence of things not seen. [2]For **by it** the elders obtained a good report. [3]**Through faith** we understand that the worlds were framed by the word of God, so that things which are seen were not made of things which do appear. [4]**By faith Abel** ... [5]**By faith Enoch** ... [6]But **without faith it is impossible to please him**: for he that cometh to God **must believe** that he is,... [7]**By faith Noah,** ... [8]**By faith Abraham,** ... [9]**By faith he** ... [11]**Through faith also Sara** ... [17]**By faith Abraham,** ... [20]**By faith Isaac** ... [21]**By faith Jacob,** ... [22]**By faith Joseph,** ... [23]**By faith Moses,** ... [24]**By faith Moses,** ... [27]**By faith he forsook Egypt** ... [28]**Through faith he kept the passover,** ... [29]**By faith they passed through the Red sea** ... [30]**By faith the walls of Jericho fell down,** ... [31]**By faith the harlot Rahab**

Hebrews 12:1-2 Wherefore seeing we also are compassed about with **so great a cloud of witnesses,** let us lay aside every weight, and the sin which doth so easily beset us, and **let us run with patience the race that is set before us,** [2]Looking unto Jesus the author and finisher of **our faith;**

If the faith they all had was imputed to them or given as the gift of God, then their example is void of meaning. Who cannot be strong in the faith if God gives you the faith to be strong? The erroneous teaching covered in this study does one thing very well; it gives those weak in faith an excuse to remain so.

1 Peter 1:7 That the **trial of your faith,** being much more precious than of gold that perisheth, though it be tried with fire, **might be found unto praise and honour and glory** at the appearing of Jesus Christ:

Why would God try your faith if he must give it to you? How could it not be found *"unto praise and honour and glory?"* The Lord deals with us, puts us through tough situations to try and build, test, and strengthen our faith in him.

There are only three things mentioned in the Scriptures that are imputed to men: iniquity, sin, and God's righteousness.

> *Psalms 32:2* Blessed is the man unto whom the LORD **imputeth not iniquity**, and in whose spirit there is no guile.

> *Romans 4:8* Blessed is the man to whom the Lord will not **impute sin**.

> *Romans 4:6* Even as David also describeth the blessedness of the man, unto whom God **imputeth righteousness** without works,

It is highly recommended you look up every one of those 231 verses in the Bible that contain the word *"faith"* before you instruct on the question here contemplated. I list a few here to let the Lord speak for himself.

> *Mark 4:40* And he said unto them, **Why are ye so fearful? How is It that ye have no faith**?

> *Luke 8:25* And he said unto them, **Where Is your faith**?

> *Matthew 9:22* But Jesus turned him about, and when he saw her, he said, Daughter, be of good comfort; **thy faith** hath made thee whole.

> *Mark 2:5* When Jesus saw **their faith**, he said unto the sick of the palsy, Son, thy sins be forgiven thee.

> *Matthew 9:29* Then touched he their eyes, saying, According to **your faith** be it unto you.

The Lord is looking for faith in man!

> *Luke 18:8* I tell you that he will avenge them speedily. Nevertheless when the Son of man cometh, **shall he find faith on the earth**?

Why would this be a question? Why would not faith be found if it must come from God?

> *Deuteronomy 32:20* And he said, I will hide my face from them, I will see what their end shall be: for they are a very froward generation, **children in whom Is no faith**.

> *Matthew 6:30* Wherefore, if God so clothe the grass of the field, which to day is, and to morrow is cast into the oven, shall he not much more clothe you, **O ye of little faith**?

If God must impart faith, what criteria or condition was not met for those whom the Lord chided for not having it? How can he reprove them for not having something he has to give them?

> *1 Thessalonians 3:10* Night and day praying exceedingly that we might see your face, and might perfect that which is **lacking in your faith**?

If your faith comes from God, how can it be lacking anything?

The faith of Jesus Christ is the corporate beliefs that the saved have concerning him. The faith of Jesus Christ is what the saved believe about him.

The Lord by himself purged our sins, but to teach that man has nothing required of him, no action to take in the course of his salvation is an error. He must repudiate his self-righteousness, admit to his helplessness, hopelessness and sinful condition and trust by faith in the gospel of the Lord Jesus Christ.

I hope that you will meditate and search the Scriptures prayerfully concerning this subject and may God be merciful and open the eyes of us all to the truth, according to his holy word, Amen.

TO THE READER

These were more noble than those in Thessalonica, in that they received the word with all readiness of mind, and searched the scriptures daily, whether those things were so.

—ACTS 17:11

It is my sincere hope, desire, and prayer that these studies will aid you in your effort to increasing your knowledge and understanding of God's word; to be better able to serve and witness his saving grace to the lost whether relative, loved one, friend, or stranger, alike.

Proverbs 24:11-12 If thou forbear to deliver them that are drawn unto death, and those that are ready to be slain; [12]If thou sayest, Behold, we knew it not; **doth not he that pondereth the heart consider it? and he that keepeth thy soul, doth not he know it? and shall not he render to every man according to his works**?

Our purpose on earth is to serve our Lord and witness his saving grace to all near and far.

As I stated at the beginning, we are in the last days and that many, even those who have never studied or read the Bible, are having their interest piqued by books and preaching on the Lord's return and the world's end. Knowing the exact time and day of his return will not make you turn to him or be a better Christian and witness for him. Knowing the doctrines and teachings of Scripture will.

Let me summarize again what I hope to have demonstrated with these studies.

1. Biblical Christianity is unique among the world's religions.

2. That there is a true Church and a False Church.

3. That there are biblical precepts that must be understood and follow if it is hoped to understand the Bible.

4. Like a puzzle, the Bible pieces must be put together a little here and a little there, line upon line, precept upon precept in building our understanding and doctrines.

5. That salvation by grace through faith is a two-part process.

6. That salvation is by God's grace through our faith at any time in history.

7. That you need the right Biblical view: Free Will, Grace/Faith, History is Open.

173

8. That two-part process of Salvation removes any supposed con-tradiction in God's plan of salvation; Christ died for all; all are eligible on the condition that they have faith toward God.

At this time in history, Church age, we have liberty in Christ from the fear of condemnation—once saved, always saved.

Feelings

For feelings come and feelings go,
And feelings are deceiving.
My warrant is the word of God
Naught else is worth believing.

Though all my heart should feel condemned,
for want of some sweet token,
There is one greater than my heart
Whose word cannot be broken.

I'll trust in God's unchanging word,
Till soul and body sever;
For though all things shall pass away
His word shall stand forever.

attri. Martin Luther (1483-1546)
German Reformer

APPENDIX

In the foreword to the book Forerunners, A History of the English Baptists lies one of the great truths of religious understanding, a description of the true Church and its false counterpart.

In this connexion, we owe a great deal to the insights of Troeltsch who, in his monumental work, The Social Teaching of the Christian Churches, has shown that from the first Christianity has shaped its life and organization according to two main patterns. ... Troeltsch calls one the Church-type and the other the Sect-type, ...For the moment we may accept the terminology of Troeltsch and with his help proceed to sketch the main features of both, ...

The most prominent feature of the Church-type is the stress it lays on the institutional character of the Church which is thought of as being in exclusive possession of the supernatural life. It thinks of the Church as the Body of Christ and as an extension of the Incarnation and, therefore, in possession of a life and tradition which carry within themselves a certain divine authority. It conveys its divine life to the individual by means of its sacramental system. Hence, it emphasizes the need of infant baptism as the sacrament of initiation which brings the child under the supernatural influence of the Church. In conformity with its sacramental character, the Church-type of Christianity usually possesses a sacerdotal ministry whose members are graded in a hierarchy. As a divine, the Church is thought of as in possession of a holiness of its own quite apart from the personal holiness of its members. For this reason, its sacraments are not rendered inefficacious by the sins of those who administer them. For the same reason, it can accept the secular order without contamination, and does not hesitate to accept State patronage and control. It endeavor's to become an integral part of the social order, utilizing the State and the ruling classes and weaving these elements into its own life, seeking to dominate the masses and thus to cover the whole life of humanity. In spite of all compromise the institution remains holy and divine. Similarly, its stability remains unaffected by the extent to which its influence over individuals is actually attained. From the masses it is content with an average level of religious and moral attainment, for it regards the highest levels of the religious life as reserved for a special class who are divinely called thereto. In so far as the Church-type aims at the stabilization of the social order and makes terms with the State in return for its patronage, it becomes dependent upon the upper classes and, therefore, conservative in its tendencies. In this way the distinction between the Church and the Kingdom of God tends to be blurred; and, for that reason, all millenarian ideas are ruled out.

The Sect-type of Christianity starts from the Christian experience of the individual believer and stresses the necessity of a genuine, if rudimentary, Christian experience in all who would join a church. No man can be born into this type of Christianity. He can enter it only by personal choice, that is, on the basis of conscious conversion. For this reason, infant-baptism frequently becomes a stumbling block, when it is retained by the Sect-type, which stands for a voluntary community whose members join it of their own free will. Thus, the Sect-type organizes itself in comparatively small groups. Being convinced that organization should follow life and not precede it, it tends to disparage the idea that the Christian community as a whole must precede the individual. It organizes itself apart from the State and is indifferent to the authority of the State and the ruling classes, whom it makes no attempt to weave into the fabric of its life. At times this attitude to the State has led to the rejection of the oath and the refusal of military service. The adherents of the Sect-type are usually drawn from the lower classes and, for this reason, it has always been more radical and democratic than the Church-type. It offers them a religion which men, who are believers and are therefore under the direct rule of Christ, can manage for themselves, instead of one managed for them by the hierarchy or the upper classes. It stands for a lay Christianity, for brotherly love and religious equality. Rejecting all sacerdotal notions, it often permits the sacraments to be administered by laymen. It tends to be critical of official spiritual guides and theologians. Its followers prefer to make their own appeal direct to the New Testament. In both range and content the asceticism of the Sect-type differs from that of the Church-type. The ascetic ideal of the former is one which is possible for all and is appointed for all, whereas that of the latter is prescribed for special classes, such as priests, monks and nuns, or for special circumstances. The Sect-type refuses to recognize a double standard of Christian living and is radical in its ethical demands, often exercising a strict discipline over all its members. It urges them all to aim at a personal, inward perfection, which is more than an average morality on good terms with the world. It calls upon its adherents to renounce the world with its pomps and pleasures. At the same time, it rejects all quasi-physical ideas of holiness, insisting that holiness is a quality not of things but only of persons, and is to be found in the common performance of the moral demands of Christ. It, therefore, takes the Sermon on the Mount seriously and, some-times, almost as a New Law. It feels compelled to reject the notion that the Church is in possession of an objective, concrete holiness, which it can impart to mankind through its sacraments and which is something quite apart from the personal holiness of its members. In its worship the Sect-type tends to revolt from ordered and liturgical forms and prefers a worship which is free, spontaneous, enthusiastic and unstylized. The tones of its piety are not aesthetic and ritualistic but ethical and prophetic....

The adherents of the Church-type have always been more numerous than those of the Sect-type. Thus arose the tendency, which has not yet spent itself, for the Church-type to regard the Sect-type as an inferior side issue or an unfortunate exaggeration or abbreviation of ecclesiastical Christianity, which alone has any right to exist. "There can, however, be no doubt," says Troeltsch, "about the actual fact: the sects, with their greater independence of the world, and their continual emphasis upon the original ideals of Christianity, often represent in a very direct and characteristic way the essential, fundamental ideas of Christianity."...Sound scholarship has made it clear that for several centuries the Christian Church fluctuated a great deal between the Church and Sect-type. Indeed, the Church-type became dominant only after Christianity had taken up into itself, from Judaism and the heathen cults, sacerdotal notions of the Christian ministry and had compromised its independence by forging an alliance with the State. It was never able completely to suppress the Sect-type which appears in the Montanists, the Novatianists, the Donatists, the Cathari, the Paulicians, the followers of Peter of Bruys, the Waldensians, the Franciscans, Wyclif and the Lollards, and the Hussites. In all these movements may be traced, in varying degrees, an attempt to assert the spirituality of the Church, an insistence that doctrines and institutions must be judged by Scripture, and also an awakening of the spirit of free lay discussion. The Paulicians, who flourished in the Eastern Church during the eighth and following centuries, and the followers of the French priest, Peter of Bruys, who lived in the twelfth century, definitely rejected infant-baptism in favour of that of believers only. ...

Forerunners, A History of the English Baptists
by A. C. Underwood, D.D.
The Baptist Union of Great Britain

ABOUT THE AUTHOR

At twenty-six, while in the USMC, Paul Walker found and accepted the salvation of the Lord Jesus Christ. He had gone twenty-six years not knowing what a Bible was other than a book with that title. It used to perplex him when he saw a magazine such as the Shooter's Bible, The Trout Fisherman's Bible, wondering what they meant. After trusting in the Lord, he read the Bible through over the next thirty days.

His Christian life had many ups and downs. Several times he was led astray by some with possibly good intentions but definitely false understanding, or application, of the Scriptures. He determined that the biggest impediment to his Christian life was not having any faithful elders in the faith to guide and counsel him, men who had labored *"in word and doctrine."*

Brother Walker determined to be a faithful elder and to help as many as he could to learn the Bible correctly. His books and studies are the fruit of that forty-three-year effort.

www.ingramcontent.com/pod-product-compliance
Lightning Source LLC
LaVergne TN
LVHW041154080426
835511LV00006B/597